Inflatable Kayaking

2014

2nd. Edition

by

Barbara Roth

Kevin Perry

Kayak Challenges Press
Copyright 2013
All rights reserved. The author and publisher take no responsibility for the use of any of the material, opinions, or methods described in this book. The name "Kayak Challenges Press" and the Kayak Challenges Press logo are trademarks of the Kayak Challenges family of companies. Published in the United States of America.

Senior Managing Editor	Kevin Perry
Technical Advisers	Kevin Perry
	Roger Curry
Cover/Book Designer	Kevin Perry
Photography	Kayleighn Price
	Barb Roth
Field Tester	CaroleAnn Perry
Wrangler	Michele Perry

Cover: CarolAnne, age 5, enjoying her first solo paddle

Reasonable questions regarding the content of this book should be addressed to:

Kayakchallenges@AOL.com

Warning: This book is not intended to replace instruction by a qualified instructor or to substitute for good personal judgment. Anyone using waterways should have an adequate working knowledge of local regulations and limitations. In using this book, the reader releases the authors from liability for any injury, including death, that might result.

Our thanks to the rehab staff of Good Samaritan Hospital, Puyallup, for helping to make our adventure possible.

And thanks to the owners of Henley's Resort at Silver Lake, Washington for helping us reach the steps *that other guy* told us we never, ever would.

Table of Contents

Introduction ix

The World of Kayaking 2

History of Inflatable Kayaks 4

Selecting a Kayak 8

Basic Skills and Equipment 34

Personal Flotation Devices 36

Safety 42

Launching 44

Paddling 46

Kayaking and the Environment 54

Kayak Rescue 56

Black River Rescue 58

Accessories 70

Repair 78

Maintenance and Storage 86

Kids and Kayaking 90

Clear Kayaking..96

Kayleighn's Story ……..98

Barb's Story …...100

Disabled Kayaking …...106

Kayak Fishing …..116

Kayak Sailing …………………………………..120

Kayak Pedaling…………………………………122

Surf Kayaking …..124

Sea Kayaking……………………………………126

Cold Weather Kayaking …………………….....130

Other Inflatables …...132

Glossary …..138

Introduction

Kayaking is an experience like no other.

For many of us the sensation of gliding across the water with your own effort is indescribable. On a quiet lake, with no noises of civilization except the occasional bark echoing across the water, your senses focus on the warmth of the sun, the coolness of the breeze, and the feel of wind caressing your skin.

You can quietly paddle on a lake or a quiet river without disturbing wildlife, observing and being observed in return.
You may be able to approach a raptor on a perfect day without disturbing it.

For a time the frustration of limitations are forgotten.

This does not require any esoteric skill. It can be done in an inflatable kayak easily with basic knowledge and respect for the limitations of yourself and your kayak.

Other kayakers may crave the visceral thrill of bashing through end-of-the-world rapids, having to use years of experience and training and top-of-the-line watercraft to navigate them safely.

Whenever we go out (on a suddenly glorious day, not a rare thing here in Puget Sound, it takes us about three minutes to cram everything into the Boatmobile and head out), either by ourselves or with our flotilla, we get lots of questions about our inflatable kayaks. Most of the questions show a basic misunderstanding of their uses and limitations.

We were at the lake one day with the girls as they tried kayaking for the first time. We were using small "recreational only" sit-on-top inflatables. These simple kayaks are safe enough to use in a protected environment under close supervision, and can be great for introducing someone to the principles of kayaking.

This guy approached us and offered $30 for one of them. He told us how he *really* wanted a kayak but couldn't afford a *good* one.

His dream had always been to paddle with the killer whales out in Puget Sound, and he felt sure he could use one of our kayaks for the experience of a lifetime.

He just couldn't understand why I didn't want to sell him one. I tried to explain that he needed something very different if he wanted to do that, that it wasn't safe.

Getting angry, he thought I was trying to sell him a more expensive kayak. He had done his research on the Internet, and he just didn't know what the big deal was about.

If it floated, it was just like the video he had seen online, and he wasn't going to be going down any rapids. He was just going to paddle around on the Sound. No big deal.

We have yet to see him on the 6 o'clock news, but it's almost inevitable if he continues in his quest and ignores facts.

I decided to write this book to answer the most frequent questions we hear, and to encourage people to try inflatables. This book is not meant to be an in-depth source of information about kayaking technique. The aim of this book is to provide an overview and basic information for people who are newcomers to kayaking, or those who are looking for non-biased information that is not easily available elsewhere.

We don't have any affiliation with any manufacturer or outfitter (other than being frequent customers) that might influence our facts or opinions.

There are so many ways to enjoy the water around us. Our goal is to introduce you to the unique joy of inflatable kayaking, and the safety principles that must go along with it.

We hope that you choose wisely and paddle safely.

The World of Kayaking

From the first moment you enter a kayak it becomes a part of you, a living extension of you that responds to every subtle movement of yours. You can feel the water as you glide through it, even the smallest waves as they hit you, and the wind as it gently nudges you. On a river you can feel the currents, and in a tidal area you can feel the pull of the ocean.

The first time you encounter this it can be pretty daunting. In a hardshell you may even capsize as you over correct to all the sensory input. In an inflatable kayak, because of it's inherent pontoon-like design, it's very difficult to tip over. You have time to relax and adapt to your new environment, and get to know the feel of the boat around you.

This inherent stability makes inflatable kayaks particularly useful for the recreational paddler (especially with kids), the fisherman, the birder, and the photographer.

Inflatables are lighter compared to hardshells, compact, and easier to store if you have limited space. They're great for traveling or if you have to carry them for any distance. They can be very inexpensive, especially for someone who wants to try kayaking but doesn't want to invest a lot of money in a hardshell.

Inflatable kayaks are (usually)easier to find than hardshells, and bear a certain stigma in some circles. The vast majority of hardshell kayaks are sold in sporting goods stores, outdoor outfitters, and dedicated kayak shops while inflatable kayaks can be found in a growing number of multi-purpose grocery stores but not so commonly in the upper-level outfitter's shops. In almost every high-end outfitter or sporting goods store you can find at least one employee who, when you ask about inflatables, will have plenty of inaccurate "facts" and a poor attitude for you.

It's not just limited to inflatables – exclusivity can by applied to almost anything if you have the (insert best word here).

One day we went into a local outfitters for some information. We were approached by this guy who was about 6 feet tall and probably weighed 47 lbs.

Now, when people look at us their first thought usually isn't "athletic couple", but this guy looked like he wanted to insist we had come in the wrong door.

We told him we were kayakers (his eyebrows shot up) and we were interested in information about some of the local rivers.

He blanched, and without looking directly at us informed us that he was an *ocean* kayaker and didn't (care to) know anything about *rivers*.

Good thing we didn't mention inflatables. We would have had to revive him.

Don't let this kind of stuff discourage you like it has for so many others.

While more and more expert providers are recognizing the value of inflatables, there is still very little useful information available at the grocery stores, discount sporting goods stores, and websites that sell the least expensive models.

The information in this book will help you make an informed decision about whether to try an inflatable kayak, which one to choose, and how to paddle safely.

History

Kayaks were first made thousands of years ago by the Inuit around the Arctic Circle. They were made by lashing together a framework of bones and driftwood and covering it with skin. The skin was dried and then waterproofed with blubber. During the summer when the sea was free of ice the men would range far from home to hunt. The word "kayak" actually means "hunter's boat".

In the 1860's John MacGregor of England became popular writing about traveling all over Europe in a boat based on an Inuit design. It was more like a canoe with a deck, and had a tent-like awning that he used in bad weather and a sail to help with propulsion.

In the 1880's George Sears became a very popular American outdoor writer with stories of paddling all over in a light-weight canoe and minimal equipment, and recreational canoeing became increasingly popular.

The popular myth is that after World War II returning GI's became famous when they began floating down the Colorado River on Army surplus inflatable bridge pontoons lashed together. Stories persist of their fearlessness and amazingly complete lack of control, fueling the image of the daredevil river-runner.

Then Sevylor was founded in France in 1948, and became successful in part with the invention of high-frequency welded PVC inflatable toys and an inflatable bathtub.

The first person to think of using one of the inflatable bathtubs may be lost in an alcoholic fog ("Hey! Jacque's passed out in that stupid bathtub thing again! Let's ……..!")

The rest, as they say, is history.

Sevylor went on to manufacture it's first kayak, the Tahiti, in 1963, and has been making the same model ever since.

The Tahiti design has been copied and modified many times since, with varying degrees of success. There are those watercraft that most resemble canoes, like the Tahiti, but also many others that are more like traditional kayaks. Their function can be utilitarian and general, or very specific and specialized. The most common characteristics are that they are inflatable, resilient, and very stable thanks to the pontoon-type sides.
    Sea Eagle, in the 1970's, started manufacturing much more durable kayaks made of polykrylar. They closely resembled the Tahiti, and are also still in production today.
    In 2007 Sevylor and Stearns, a maker of a well-designed and reasonably durable line of kayaks, the IK's, was acquired by Coleman (a subsidiary of Zodiac) and their lines were merged and designs modified (except for the Tahiti, which still remains unchanged).
    The majority of changes in inflatable watercraft

construction have had to do with the materials that are used to make the kayaks to go along with new engineering techniques and designs. Companies like Aire and Maxxon now make kayaks made of bonded materials that are nearly indestructible.

Aire, for instance, offers a 10 year warranty, and often waives that depending on the problem. They are used by most rental companies, and that says something in this litigious society.

Some manufacturers have focused on meeting customers' other needs. It may not seem like much, but ways to attach gear, storage, and other "user-friendly" improvements to a plain hull have made kayaking much more enjoyable for the casual paddler

A paddle holder can be very useful along with a mesh storage bag, deck bungee cording, and a waterproof bag that attaches to the clips built into the hull :

.

Notes:

Selecting a kayak

Anyone in the market for an inflatable kayak today faces a bewildering array of choices.

There are countless promises, endless razzledazzle, and baffling liberties of language taken by marketing types. You may find all kinds of names for the same thing, all meant to add glamour to pedestrian parts, or to rename something that may have a less-than-stellar reputation.

Do your homework! Clever or lurid marketing should not prevent you from doing extensive research (such as studying this book) and learning as many facts as possible. Remember, your safety (and perhaps the safety of your family) can be dependent on what you decide.

There are independent sites that offer reviews of many of the inflatable kayaks today. Paddling.net, kayakreview.org/inflatable-kayaks, and inflatablekayakworld.com are three websites that offer a lot of information.

When shopping for an inflatable kayak you need to make a clear and honest statement of what you want to do, where you want to do it, and if you can do it when you get there.

What made you decide to look for an inflatable kayak? Was it low initial cost, convenience (not having to lug around a hardshell), lack of space, or did a friend recommend one?

You may have decided on an inflatable as the most inexpensive introduction to kayaking, and I hope we can help you make the best choice possible to choose a kayak that will serve you well for many years.

There's a myriad of styles and materials which dictate the function and cost of an inflatable. You may see "certification" by the National Marine Manufacturer's Association (NMMA) on any kayak you see that has been manufactured in the US. The certification standards are determined by the manufacturers of the kayaks that are certified, if that has any significance for you.

Less expensive watercraft tend to be less durable and more prone to punctures. Some kayaks to be aware of are made of the same material, quality, and thickness of the air mattress sold next to them in the grocery store. As a general rule of thumb, kayaks that retail for under $200 are only safe for use in protected waters. They are usually made of a comparatively thin single thickness of PVC and often have (cheap) poorly functional air valves to keep down costs.

Sevylor touts their venerable K79 kayak as having navigated some of the greatest rivers in the world. It's easy to do with a large support team and deep water far from the banks and sharp objects. It's not so easy to do with an angry pre-teen who's been dragged away from his video games, whose single goal in life now seems to be to impale your kayak on any available branch.

With good judgment and some luck these boats can actually last some time, but you have to resist the temptation to try to use them in situations for which they may not be safe.

There's a new "environmentally friendly" material being used on some inflatables. It's called "thermoplastic polyurethane". The manufacturer claims it is tough and puncture-resistant, but I haven't been able to find any independent evaluation of its qualities.

Even slightly more expensive kayaks can be much more durable and can be abused (within reason) with minimal risk for serious damage or compromising safety.

Sea Eagle is an example of a reasonable compromise between cost and durability. Their proprietary "polykrylar" is a tough, lightweight hull material that can take a beating.

Many of the kayaks being manufactured now have one hull thickness made up of multiple layers of material (such as nylon or polyester) and PVC. The hull serves as a high pressure air chamber, providing stiffness (and improved performance).

These can be some of the highest-quality (and most expensive) kayaks available. For example, AIRE uses hypalon (the same material in Zodiac and other indestructible inflatable boats), and Innova uses nytralon, a nylon-based, environmentally-friendly material that is also nearly indestructible, but heavier.

Other, so-called "bladder boats", have a hull made of multiple layers of material that encase a separate single-layer PVC air bladder. These are very durable (besides the tough outer hull the air bladder may be 30g PVC, compared to the 26g hull of the K79), but may not be able to contain high air pressure. To help with stiffness some manufactures use a "drop-stitch" floor that will take two or three psi (three times the pressure of typical low pressure air bladders). These kayaks take much longer to dry than single-thickness (whatever the material may be) kayaks – something to keep in mind if you don't have someplace to safely keep them while they dry out before putting them away.

Fabric used for bladder boat hulls is usually measured in "deniers" – designating the weight and thickness of the fabric used. The higher the denier, the greater the weight, durability, resistance to tears, and price.

A fabric with a denier of 1200 or more is extremely tough, and used on high-end kayaks.

Fabric with a denier of 800 – 1200 is reasonable durable, and is usually found on mid-priced kayaks, or those meant for some restrained antics.

Any fabric with a denier of less than 800 should be viewed with some suspicion. It may only be for show, or a false sense of security.

Hypalon is a type of synthetic rubber that's been used for higher-echelon kayaks for years. It's resistant to chemicals, salt water, oxidation, ultraviolet light, and extreme temperatures. When stored, it won't develop permanent creases.

However, it's heavier than PVC, the fabric is more expensive, and each piece of the kayak has to be glued by hand. Repairs can be difficult and expensive.

The newest material for eco-friendly paddlers is a polyester ripstop fabric. It is light and durable, and usually treated with something on the inside to prevent any air loss and something like Teflon on the outside to help with repelling water and stain prevention.

At the time of this writing Advanced Elements (an

excellent PackLite) and Innova/Gumotex use this in some of their kayaks, and it is sure to become more popular (and less expensive) in the next couple of years.

Always keep in mind that all inflatables, very much like cars, are not created equal, even if the cost is the same. Some companies offer kayak models in Europe or the Far East that are not available in the U.S. In some cases it has to do with a company not having the resources for world-wide distribution, in some cases it's a matter of merely changing the name or amenities, and in others it may be that the kayaks may not meet local standards.

We have one kayak that was actually run over by a bus. The only damage done is repeatedly trying to explain the tread marks and enduring the snickers ("Where exactly were you paddling that you got hit by a *bus*?")

We had another kayak that cost about the same, but it didn't survive one close encounter with a six year old.

Just like cars, some kayak manufacturers use different components to save costs. For example, there is a variety of air valves commonly used for inflatable kayaks (but be careful – pump adapters can be specific for air valves. You may not be able fill up your kayak if you have the wrong adaptr). There are only a couple of basic valves, but the marketing types can be very creative when using cutesy names to try and sound like they've got something new and perfect.

The cheapest inflatables use a "plug" or "pinch" valve to save money (and lower the cost of the kayak). If you see them, take a pass and look for something better. They can be very difficult to use. They limit the amount of air you can force through the valve, and therefore the speed of inflation. They often fail to work "one way" so you must insert the cap very quickly after you remove the pump nozzle or lose air pressure. Once you have the valve stoppered the cap may pop off, and you lose air pressure. The valve can easily wear out, and you will have a permanent leak. The plastic arm that attaches the cap to the kayak may break and chances are you will lose the cap. If the air chamber does hold air as long as you want it to, it will take what seems forever to deflate a large air chamber through such a small valve, especially if it actually works "one-way" and you have to hold it open so the air chamber can empty.

Sevylor recently has started using "Double Lock Fast Valves" – a euphemism for a slightly improved pinch-type valve. The aperture is larger, so filling/deflating time is faster. When the fill tube is pressed down it closes off the valve after you've filled the air chamber, then a plug /cap on a plastic arm seals off the fill tube (hence the "double lock").

Unfortunately, the large lip on the cap can easily get caught on something and flip the valve up and the cap off, causing the air chamber to deflate suddenly. On some of the kayaks I've seen these valves have been repositioned to be out of the way, but the possibility still exists. Mr. Murphy and his Law would insist that you take this into account when trying to decide which kayak to choose.

Lower level kayaks usually use a combination of plug valves and two-part "Boston" valves.

The Boston valve is simplicity itself. The top cap unscrews to uncover the valve body, and the pump adapter is inserted in the valve aperture. There is a small rubber diaphragm at the other end of the valve (inside the kayak) that allows air in and blocks it from escaping. Either a foot pump or hand pump can be used, with or without a gauge. They're fairly reliable, and easily replaced. Next-level kayaks may have Boston valves exclusively.

The highest quality tier of kayaks have high-pressure air

chambers. They use several different types of air valves that can take the force that Boston valves cannot (the newest kayaks at this writing are pressurized at 6.5 psi – something thought almost Impossible several years ago, resulting in amazing hull rigidity). Halkey-Roberts ("military") valves are the most common, and require a special adapter. They are elegantly simple. The central plunger includes a plastic plate and gasket at the end and is spring-loaded to maintain an adequate air seal.

Before you decide on a kayak, you need to determine exactly what you want to use it for. What types of water recreation do you have locally? Or, if you're planning on traveling, what kind of kayaking do you plan to do as part of your trip? Paddling on a lake or a slow, wide river takes a very different kind of kayak and paddling technique than one designed for white water.

Exploring backwaters and swamps calls for a very different kayak than one you would use on a large lake.

There is a wide range of kayaks meant for flatwater. They tend to be longer and are designed to travel (track) in a straight line.

To do that some manufacturers claim that their "tubular floors" that run from bow to stern keep the kayak pointed forward when paddling. This may be true, but difficult to prove in practice.   To actually contribute to directional stability and make it
 easier to paddle, some manufactures add some sort of skeg (a blade-like structure) or a strake (not as deep, but longer):

There are single (K1), tandem (K2, meant for two), and even longer types meant for three or more. Parents with smaller children can find the longer kayaks very useful for enjoying the water with their kids.

There are many multi-purpose boats that are engineered with compromises that serve both pretty well. They may not paddle in a straight line as easily as the specialized flatwater boats, and they may not turn as quickly as whitewater kayaks, but with practice a paddler can enjoy directional stability. Someone who doesn't demand a lot can find the same kayak will work very well in Class II or even Class III rapids.

Kayaks that are designed for very demanding whitewater are nimble and extremely durable. They can be difficult to paddle in a straight line (many have little or no strakes or skegs), but are great for the quick maneuvers that heavy whitewater demands, and the tricks that some kayakers perform. They usually have a pronounced "rocker" (raised bow and stern) that helps them maneuver over obstacles. They also tend to be short and sleek.

A growing number of manufacturers are adding removable skegs to their products – use the skeg on flatwater, take it off if you're going to be scraping over rocks in whitewater. It adds another dimension to the kayak, making it more truly "multi-purpose".

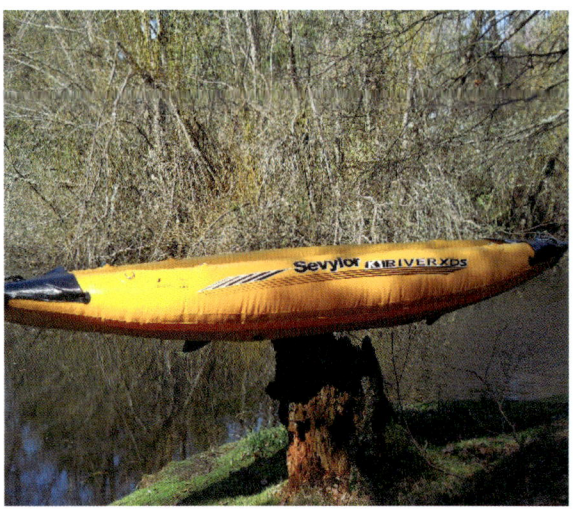

Kayaks may be open, or closed in with a sprayskirt that fits snugly around your waist and the cockpit opening. It's designed to keep water out, since there may be no way for the water to escape from inside the craft. Too much water in the kayak will greatly affect performance. If you do choose a closed-cockpit kayak, there is a very specific skill set you need to know for safety. We strongly suggest you take lessons from a local professional to learn how to paddle safely in one of these wonderful kayaks before using it.

Some whitewater kayaks, especially those that are open, are "self-bailing". This means there is at least one opening in the floor that can let excess water out that splashes into the boat in heavy whitewater or surf conditions. The opening can be capped during calm conditions when water won't accumulate in the kayak, preventing any water from entering through the floor.

The floor valve can be very useful when washing your kayak after you use it. Soapy water can be drained more easily from the inside of the kayak, reducing drying time. Or, you can spend your afternoon tipping the kayak back and forth, getting frustrated and tired trying to get the water out. Just remember to cap the valve when you're done, or you'll discover a kayak with some really disgusting water the next time you take it out.

A very close cousin of whitewater kayaks are those meant for surf. They can be open or sit-on-top, usually with sharply squared-off hulls to help cut into the water for better maneuvering.

"Sea kayaks" are at the other end of the performance spectrum. They tend to be long and narrow, displacing a comparatively large amount of water. They move quickly and gracefully through the water, best in a straight line. They aren't meant to be nimble and turn quickly, they are meant to cover very large areas of water with relative ease. They usually come equipped with a sprayskirt as well because of the likelihood of water spilling over the deck.

You should always keep comfort in mind when choosing a kayak. If you're not comfortable in what you've chosen, you won't enjoy your time on the water and you'll end up being disappointed and getting rid of it.

Comfort involves "fit". Some kayaks have very narrow cockpits, others have wider openings that larger paddlers will fit in much more comfortably.

With a closed cockpit your legs should fit inside comfortably. If there is a foot brace you should be able to reach it easily.

If you find yourself with a kayak that has a narrow cockpit that is uncomfortable you can add a padded cooler or tackle box just behind the seat to widen the space between the air tubes to make extra room. Just be careful to not widen it too much and distort the shape of the kayak, or cause any chafing against the air tube wall.

If the cockpit is too wide you may find yourself sliding around. You can add foam pads on each side to make your position stable but comfortable.

If you're "altitude challenged" your ability to reach over the

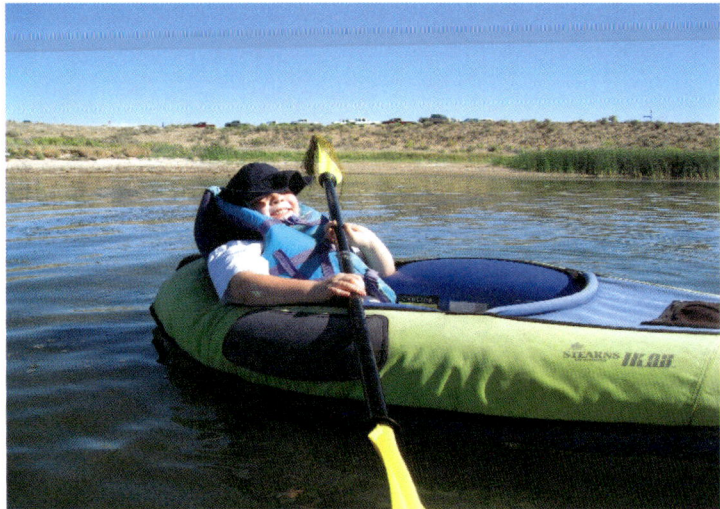

sides could be compromised, and you could be uncomfortable trying to paddle. It may be fun for a while, but in the end you would probably have to cut your day short and return home disappointed, tired, and sore.

You can slip something under the seat to help you function above the gunwales, but be very careful about changing the center of gravity – sitting too high can make the kayak very "tippy".

You should be able to sit snugly but not tightly and paddle comfortably. Your feet and legs should not be forced into any uncomfortable positions, whether in an open or closed cockpit. You should be able to enter and exit easily and gracefully. If it has a closed cockpit it should not impinge on you in any way, and if a sprayskirt is included it should fit snugly so that it is essentially watertight. It should be taut so no water will pool in a dip between you and the kayak deck.

How much time do you plan to spend in your kayak? If your goal is lazy afternoons on a lake or a quiet river, a smaller, undemanding kayak may serve you very well. A large inflatable can be heavy and difficult to carry and paddle for the person who only occasionally gets out on the water.

If you're planning on frequently spending all day on the water fishing, or several days camping, be sure to plan for it by choosing a kayak that has plenty of storage for your gear and greater durability, and comfortable seats.

Are you going to be kayaking alone, as a couple, or in a group? There are tandem kayaks that can also work very well as a single. There are also some "tandem" kayaks that seem meant for hobbits. If you are going to choose a tandem, make sure it will have enough room for both of you, "room" having several implications (remember how things went when you attempted to put up Christmas lights together for the first time?).

A tandem can be a great choice for two paddlers of different skill levels. The stronger paddler can take over if the other paddler becomes tired.

If you're planning to be a part of a group, talk with the people in the group to get their input. At least at first, you want to match your capabilities and your kayak's characteristics with theirs.

Last but not least, most people have to consider cost vs. budget.

More than most things, with kayaks you usually get what you pay for. Costs can range from less than $100 to several thousands, determined by materials used, accessories included, and esoteric function.

If you buy the cheapest boat you can find, you won't *ever* be happy with it. It may only last a short time before developing a leak, or be difficult to handle (ever try to grab smooth, wet plastic toy, or maybe a wet toddler, without it slipping?). It may be difficult to paddle, especially in a straight line. You'll be disappointed and will miss the opportunity to enjoy a lifetime of paddling. Spending a little more for the kayak that best meets your needs will be the best investment of your life. You can get a kayak that may last you and your family forever.

We have had some kayaks that were more than 30 years old (and were mid-level when they were manufactured) that are still useable on mild water. They've lasted this long because they've been used in the manner they were designed for, and well-taken care of.

Used inflatable kayaks can be found online in classifieds such as Craigslist, auction sites such as ebay, and yard sales, and on billboards, and at some outfitters. You may find a great deal, or a disaster. The seller may be getting rid of it because it's a terrible kayak, or could be upgrading to a better one. Be sure to ask where it was used, and, maybe more importantly, where it wasn't.

Look for signs of wear versus abuse or neglect. Heavy use will show with deep scrape marks on the hull or floor. Abuse may show as crusted dirt or stains, fading or discoloration..

Make sure all seams are intact. If all the seams are glued, look for sloppy gluing that may have been done during repair efforts.

If parts of the hull are sewn together, look for thread unraveling. Seams are notoriously difficult to patch successfully, and the owner may have tried it, not fixed the leak, and decided to make it someone else's problem.

Some seams can actually be welded back together. Kits are available on Amazon and other retailers. It takes some practice and skill, but it can be done.

Look for sloppy patches, or a lot of them. What could they have been doing with the kayak that has required so much repair? Run, don't walk, away from something like that. Some leaky patches can be safely removed and the hole re-patched successfully, but the process can be labor-intensive and, in the end, not worth it. Be realistic, not optimistic.

Keep in mind that any repair compromises the integrity of the hull. You may find that your patch isn't successful at the worst possible time.

Beware of severe fading. UV light can cause severe deterioration of the components of the kayak, and may not manifest itself until later, when it simply falls apart.

Mildew or other stains can indicate that the kayak was not treated properly. It could have been put away wet, or not cleaned and washed after use. Mildew may eventually compromise the integrity of the hull and/or air bladder.

Examine the carrying case, if there is one. Does it show signs of significant wear? It there's not one, where was the kayak stored unprotected? Being carried in the trunk of a car or the back of a truck can cause isolated wear and weakening of the hull. If the kayak has been stored without any protection, was it resting on or against any sharp objects that may have caused a weakening in the hull?

Storage bags are easy to find, and a great investment. They're available from manufacturers and outfitters for a price, or something just as functional but not as pretty can be found at military surplus stores. Make sure it will be durable enough to protect the kayak for the conditions you'll be subjecting it to.

It's common sense, but, despite what the marketing descriptions may say, a kayak made of a single thickness, about the same as an air mattress and costing $100, is not as durable, or safe, as a boat made of multiple layers of ballistic-grade nylon and 32g PVC or a single layer of hypalon that costs $1000.

Something in between will probably meet your needs. You have to determine, knowledgeably and objectively, what kayak that may be.

I've formulated a table to attempt a rough comparison of most of the inflatable kayaks available today. Rated on a number of 1 to 10 (10 being the best), the scores take into account function, quality, durability, versatility, comfort, cost, customer service/ factory support, handling/storage, and just plain fun.

No model meets every need, or every budget. Most of these we've labeled "multi-purpose" because, essentially, that's what they are. Their characteristics lend them to some activities more than others, and it's up to you to decide which kayak matches to the paddling you'll be doing.

We've also tried to identify those models that lend themselves best to one or two specific purposes.

I've tried to list them according to quality, but there are so many factors involved I found it to be impossible, so in many instances I've just grouped most of the kayaks offered by the same manufacturer together and let you research what characteristics make the difference.

A big factor is cost. Generally, $1500 for a kayak you'll only use occasionally on a lake or mild whitewater is not "consumer friendly", no matter what it's quality is. There are probably better choices you can make.

For instance, my fiance's everyday kayak is actually a canoe. It's wider, therefore even more stable (for standing up) than a "kayak", with a corresponding heavier weight capacity (450 lbs) for carrying more gear than a comparable kayak. It has a durable hull with lots of D-rings for securing gear, and a reasonable price. It's not as nimble as some of the kayaks, and not as expensive as some others. There's room for a dog or a child, and has a color that won't show too much dirt and mud.

Another kayak we have is long and narrow, and can accommodate several adults, kids, and gear, but is a little tippy.

Every buyer has to determine what their needs are and how much they want to spend.

Please note: This table is by no means complete. There are many kayaks that we have not been able to evaluate (yet!). We will add information as it becomes available to us.

Single Kayaks		Score
Intex Challenger 1	recreational only	2
Coleman SOT	recreation only, kids	3
Sevylor QuikPak 3 Coverless K1 SOT	recreational only, kids	
Airhead Baja	flatwater, surf, kids	3
Sevylor QuikPak Covered K3 SOT	flatwater, surf, kids disabled	4
Sevylor K5 Kiowa	flatwater, kids, fishing	3.5
Airhead Montana	multi-purpose	5
Coleman Exponent Fastback	multi-purpose	5
Qayak	multi-purpose	5
Advanced Elements Firefly	beginner, flatwater kids	5.5
Advanced Elements Advanced Frame	multi-purpose	7
Advanced Elements Advanced Frame Sport	multi-purpose	7

Advanced Elements Lagoon 1	flatwater, calm rivers teenagers	6
Stearns IK 84	kids, flatwater	5
Stearns IK 96	kids, teens, flatwater	5.5
Stearns IK 116	multi-purpose	6
Advanced Elements Packlite	backpacking, travel flatwater, calm rivers, kids	7.5
Infinity Orbit 245	multi-purpose, travel	6
Bic Yakka 80	multi-purpose	6
Sevylor XK1	whitewater, surf	7
Sevylor Rio Canoe KCC 305	multi-purpose	7
Sevylor QuickPak 5	flatwater, mild whitewater	6
Sevylor Coral Sea	flatwater, fishing, diving	6
Aquaglide Columbia One HB	multi-purpose	6
Aquaglide Deschutes One HB	multi-purpose	6.5
Swimline Flash	multi-purpose	5

Bic Yakka 120	multi-purpose	6
Bic Yakkair 1	multi-purpose	6
Advanced Frame Expedition	ocean, multi-purpose	8
Advanced Element StraitEdge	ocean, rivers	7
Sea Eagle 300x	whitewater, multi-purpose, travel	7
Zoik AlterEgo 1	multi-purpose	7
Advanced Elements AirFusion	multi-purpose	7
Tributary Strike 1	multi-purpose	6
Tributary Tomcat	multi-purpose	7
Tributary Tomcat LV	travel, playboat, kids	6.5
Tributary Sawtooth I	multi-purpose	6.5
Hobie i9S	sailing, flatwater	6
Hobie i12S	sailing, flatwater	6
Innova (Gumotex) Solar	flatwater, ocean	7
Innova Helios	multi-purpose	7

Innova (Gumotex) Safari	whitewater, ocean/surf, travel	7.5
Innova Twist	multi-purpose, travel	6.5
Innova Swing I	mild whitewater, backpacking, advanced kids	7
NRS RIKEN Seminole I	whitewater	6
NRS Bandit 1	whitewater (Class IV)	6.5
NRS Rascal	whitewater, kids	7
NRS MaverIK I	multi-purpose	6.5
NRS MaverIK Performance Package	whitewater	6.5
NRS Outlaw I	multi-purpose/whitewater	6.75
NRS Pike fishing IK	fishing, touring	7.5
Innova Traveller	advanced whitewater	7
Innova Seaker	sea touring	7
Hyside Padillac K1	whitewater	7
Incept Explorer	whitewater	6
Airis Play Single SOT	multi-purpose stunts, travel, disabled	7

Saturn AirFast	multi-purpose, disabled	7
Saturn TK 365 Catamaran hull	multi-purpose, racing	7
Airis Sport	multi-purpose, backpacking, travel, disabled, kids	7
Airis Angler SOT	fishing, birding, photography disabled	8
Aire Force	Serious whitewater, surf	7
Aire Lynx I	multi-purpose	7.5
Aire Outfitter I	multi-purpose/whitewater	7
Zoik Alter Ego I	multi-purpose	7
Zoik Ego Trip SOT/SUP	flatwater, some whitewater, surf	6
Zoik RF I	multi-purpose	7

Tandem kayaks		Score
Sevylor Fiji	recreation	2
Intex Challenger 2	recreation	2.5
Sevylor Tahiti K79	flatwater, calm rivers	3
Friday Harbor	flatwater, calm rivers	3
Aquaglide Yakima	flatwater, calm rivers	3.5
Aquaglide Rogue SOT	flatwater, calm rivers disabled, diving	4.5
Sevylor Ranger Krc 79	multi-purpose	4
Maxxon Rendevoux	flatwater, calm rivers	4
Intex Explorer 2	multi-purpose	5
Sea Eagle 330	day trips, multi-purpose	5
Sea Eagle 370	day trips, multi-purpose	6
Sea Eagle 380x	multi-purpose, whitewater	7
Sea Eagle 420x	multi-purpose, whitewater, Family	7
Sea Eagle 385 FT	multi-purpose, touring fishing	7.5

Airhead Roatan	flatwater	4
Airhead Montana 2	multi-purpose	6
Sevylor Pointer K2	multi-purpose	6
Sevylor Yukon KCC 380	multi-purpose	5.5
Sevylor Tandem SOT	flatwater, beginner disabled	5
Sevylor Adventure Canoe	multi-purpose, camping	6
Sevylor Adventure Plus Canoe	multi-purpose, family, camping	6.5
Sevylor Colorado Canoe KCC335	multi-purpose	6
Sevylor Hudson KCC 360	multi-purpose, family	6.5
Sevylor Pacific 500 SKS 500	multi-purpose, family,	7.5
Swimline Trekker	multi-purpose	5
Swimline Traveller	SOT, multi-purpose	5
Swimline Flash 2	multi-purpose	5
Pathfinder Tandem	multi-purpose, family	6.5
Conquest Dyad	family, reef exploration	6.5

Advanced Elements Lagoon 2	multi-purpose	6
Infinity Odyssey 295	multi-purpose	7
Infinity Odyssey 375	family, camping	7
Z-Pro Tango	multi-purpose	6.5
Advanced Elements Advanced Frame Convertible	multi-purpose, family	8
Advanced Elements StraitEdge 2	multi-purpose, family	7
Advanced Elements Canoe	multi-purpose, family camping	7
Stearns IC 140 Canoe	multi-purpose, family camping	6
Stearns IK 140	multi-purpose	6.5
Bic Kalyma	multi-purpose, disabled	7
Maxxon Mk 1205	multi-purpose	8
Maxxon Cayman II	multi-purpose	8
Maxxon Cayman III	multi-purpose	8
Maxxon Express II	multi-purpose	7

Maxxon Katatumbo II	Same as Express II	
NRS Outlaw II	whitewater	6.5
NRS MaverIK II	multi-purpose	6.5
Tributary Strike 2	multi-purpose	8
Tributary Tomcat Tandem	multi-purpose	8
Tributary Sawtooth 2	flatwater, touring	8
Airis Play Tandem	multi-purpose, disabled, travel	8
Hobie i14S	sailing, flatwater	6.5
Innova (Gumotex) Helios 2	multi-purpose	8
Innova Sunny	multi-purpose	8
Innova Swing 2	multi-purpose, travel	7
Innova Vagabond Canoe	multi-purpose, family, camping	7
Innova Orinoco Canoe	whitewater	6
RMR IK-123	whitewater	6
B.P. Trinity	whitewater	6
B.P. Trinity II	whitewater, camping	6.5

	travel	
Sea Eagle PaddleSki	multi-purpose, sailing	7
Bic Yakkair 2	multi-purpose	7
Aquaglide Columbia Tandem HB	touring	7.5
Aquaglide Deschutes Tandem HB	multi-purpose	7.5
Sevylor XK2	multi-purpose	7
Sevylor XK17	Ocean, touring	8
Aire Lynx II	multi-purpose	8
Aire Outfitter II	multi-purpose	7.5
Aire Sea Tiger	ocean touring	7
Aire Traveller Canoe	multi-purpose, family, camping	7
Aire Transom Traveller Canoe	multi-purpose, camping family	7
Grand A380 Canoe	multi-purpose	7
Grand A380P Canoe (Professional)	multi-purpose, whitewater	7.5
Grand A450	multi-purpose, family	7.5

Canoe	camping	
Grand A450P Canoe (Professional)	multi-purpose, family camping	8
Saturn 12' Expedition	multi-purpose, family camping	7
Saturn 13' Expedition	multi-purpose, family camping	7.5
Saturn 13' Whitewater	whitewater, family, camping	7.5
Saturn KaBoat 12' Motor Canoe	multi-purpose, camping, family	8
Saturn KaBoat 14' Motor Canoe	multi-purpose, camping, family	8.5
Saturn KaBoat 16' Motor Canoe	multi-purpose, camping family, touring	8.5
Saturn Pro-Angler	multi-purpose, family fishing	9
Zoik Alter Ego II	multi-purpose	8
Zoik RF II	multi-purpose	8

There's not one "right" kayak for every person, or every situation. Choose a kayak fits your budget, your skill level, and your paddling goals, that's comfortable and fun to paddle, and leaves room for your paddling skills to grow.

Notes:

Basic Skills/Requirements

You need to know how to swim.

It should be common sense, but every year you hear about someone who got out on the water in a situation that required that they know how to swim, and couldn't, and got into trouble. Hindsight may be 20/20, but some situations have obvious demands.

You need to know your limits. If you are in water in a lake that is waist deep and you're with a group of experienced swimmers, and they know you can't swim and are willing to make sure you're going to be OK, then you might have reason to feel safe.

If you are in a kayak and you don't know how to swim, and you're away from shore and putting all your confidence in your PFD to keep you safe, you're in trouble.

If you are in a kayak and you don't know how to swim, you are in danger if you decide to paddle down a river of any kind, no matter who you are with.

Before you attempt any excursion, you need to practice entering and exiting your kayak, paddling, and turning. This will get you comfortable with your kayak, give you basic skills, and the confidence to react to any adverse circumstances.

Basic rules for safe kayaking include:

Always go with an experienced friend.

Always paddle in a group of at least three (one to get into trouble, one to stay with that person, and the third to go for help. Only in groups of four or more can you have some designated to have hysterics).

Always have all the safety equipment you need.

Always tell someone where you're going and when you plan to return.

Always make sure the water you're going to be on is safe for you.

Be able to paddle
Be able to balance

Those with disabilities can enjoy kayaking, (see the appropriate chapter) but you must be able to use your hips and lower body to maintain balance.

For those who have inflatables with closed cockpits – I strongly suggest lessons from local professionals. You'll learn more than you can imagine.

Notes:

Personal Floatation Devices

A PFD, or personal floatation device, is part of the equation that will determine if your time on the water will be wonderful or dreadful.

It's simple, but true: YOUR PFD WILL NOT HELP YOU AT ALL IF YOU'RE NOT WEARING IT.

That's the reason the U.S. Coast Guard (and similar entities around the world) determine what kind of and how many PFD's are necessary for different water-related activities. Check with your local authorities before you start planning your time on the water to make sure you comply with local rules and requirements.

Remember, YOUR PFD WILL NOT HELP YOU AT ALL IF YOU'RE NOT WEARING IT.

PFD's come in all kinds of sizes, shapes, colors, and materials, usually determined by its intended use.

Depending on weight and body type, most adults only need an extra seven to twelve pounds of buoyancy to keep their head above water. A very low percentage of body fat may require more buoyancy (does anyone still remember Joe Frazier, the championship boxer with *no* body fat, sinking straight to the bottom of the pool when he tried to swim on national TV years ago?).

Other factors that may affect how much "extra lift" you would need include lung size, clothing, items in your pockets or attached to your device, and whether the water is smooth or rough. A PFD may act very differently in rough or fast-moving water than in a calm lake. Pockets full of change or other heavy items may make the difference between keeping your head above water or not.

You should try out a PFD before you need it if you can. If you go to a large sporting goods store, there should be a wide selection. Take your time and try on as many as you like – it's *your* life at stake, and it deserves the time and attention you need to make the right decision (if they won't let you try out as many as you want, they obviously aren't interested in your repeat business). It should fit snugly and keep your face comfortably above water level while not riding up. You should not be able to slip out of it (which may occur if your stomach is appreciably larger than your chest). If any of this happens, get a different PFD. The one you tried won't do you any good.

Make sure you read the label on any PFD you're contemplating using to be sure it's meant for someone with your weight and size.

Types

Some full-body suits are meant to protect you from cold water (worn by deep-sea fishermen and others who spend their time in cold waters). They're specialty items you may never see unless you're a fan of "The Deadliest Catch" or something similar on TV.

Type I Life Jackets are bulky vests. They're meant for situations where rescue may be hours away while the wearer is in rough or open water. They are usually a highly visible color, and are not designed for any activity other than floating.

The awkward orange Type II "life jackets" you see on

cruise ships in the movies, with the big pads on your chest and the huge horse collar, are designed to keep your head above water, especially if you're unconscious.

They may be inflatable, and are now designated as Near

Shore Buoyant Vests. They are meant to be worn for a short time only. You can swim or participate in other activities while wearing them, but they can be uncomfortable. Because they're cheap, they can be seen most often on kids. They are not particularly suited for paddling.

Ski vests are more adjustable, and are designed to fit very snugly. They are great if you're holding your arms out straight in front of you while standing, but don't allow for a lot of arm and shoulder movement.

They're inexpensive and easy to find. They're engineered to protect you from sudden impact with the water, not strenuous activity. Good paddling PFD's are lined with material to wick moisture away. They can be used by the casual paddler for a short time, but can become very uncomfortable, restrictive, sweaty, and miserable after a short time of active paddling.

Paddling vests have evolved from ski vests. They are designed to allow the wearer to move their arms and shoulders freely while sitting. There are usually adjustments not only at the abdomen and chest, but also the shoulders. The better models are lined with neoprene or a similar substance that is more comfortable if you're sweating a lot.

With the growing interest in kayak fishing, more paddling vests are being made with multiple pockets and attachment points, handy for a whistle, compass, camera, or other equipment that is not too heavy. This particular vest has a heavy-duty zipper instead of buckles, with a small pouch that attaches over it. Note the pockets, loops, and ring.

With all the pockets and pouches, you have to be careful not to overload the buoyancy effect of the vest. For instance,

tucking a firearm in one of the pockets would probably seriously affect the function of the PFD (and if you feel the need to carry a firearm where you're going to be paddling, you might want to consider an alternative site).

If you've tried everything and still can't find a PFD that doesn't slip off when you're in the water, look for one that has a belt (or you can add one to "perfect" PFD except for that pesky slipping off thing) that attaches in the back, goes down between your legs, and then buckles to the front. It doesn't have to be tight (and uncomfortable) but it has to be able to keep the PFD from slipping up and off.

Another alternative might be the new generation of inflatable PFD's. They come in an increasing number of variations of vests, fanny packs, and other configurations. They're easy to wear and at least as safe as comparable traditional PFD's.

One complaint is that the "arming" mechanism is expensive. If you have to use it, you should be happy to be around to pay the price afterward.

If you have one for your child, try to impress on him or her that just letting it inflate for entertainment is not such a great idea.

Care and Maintenance

Don't alter or modify your PFD (except for the belt I just discussed). It's designed to work a certain way, and changing it may decrease its function significantly.

PFD's lose their buoyancy when crushed. Don't sit or kneel on it, use it as a bludgeon, or place heavy objects on it. Don't store it stuffed into a tight container with other PFD's.

Wash it and let it dry thoroughly before storing it. Metal parts will rust or corrode, sand will become permanently embedded in velcro. Don't place it near any direct source of heat that may melt or weaken the material. Mildew and mold may also weaken the fabric. Even it doesn't affect it's function, but it may make you reluctant to wear it.

Use a zipper cleaner/lubricant (yes there is such a thing) to keep the zippers from seizing.

Check your PFD before every use to make sure there are no tears or holes, and that all seams, straps, and hardware are intact.

Sunlight can be just as destructive of your PFD as your kayak. Fading can indicate loss of strength or integrity. Before you put it on, test your PFD by tugging sharply on straps and hardware to make sure it will be safe in an emergency. It should be stored in the same cool, dry place as your inflatable.

Notes:

More notes:

Safety

Before getting on the water, there are several factors you need to be aware of.

First and foremost, remember that other people will usually be the most dangerous environmental element you will encounter. You will be in a small craft that may be difficult to see by larger boats. Some people on personal water craft (such as jet skis) may consider harassing you as entertainment.

You should always know where you're launching from, where you're going, and, most importantly, where you're getting out of the water. Be sure you can easily identify your "take-out" *from the water* or you may have a very difficult ending to a wonderful day ("Well, I *thought* it was *here*. Have any idea where we are?").

Always check weather conditions for the time you'll be on the water. Inflatables ride on top of the water, which makes them especially susceptible to wind and waves. Windy conditions can make the danger of hypothermia (the dangerous lowering of body temperature) much worse, and cause rough water conditions that may lead to swamping or capsizing.

Water temperature may be very important to the outcome of your day.

Last week here in Northwest Washington the trail temperature next to one of the rivers was 108F. The water temperature in the snow-melt fed river was 33F. Any spill in water that cold would immediately cause hypothermia. Sudden immersion in cold water causes the automatic reflex of gasping – if your face is in the water, you'll inhale icy water, endangering your life.

Launching into a bay or surf could have the same effect if you haven't taken the necessary precautions to prevent hypothermia, such as dressing in layers with the outermost layer being waterproof.

Some insidious effects of hypothermia are judgment impairment and slowing reflexes. If you gradually develop hypothermia because you've been out on the water for some time and you become chilled, you may not realize how cold you've become, and how much you need to warm up.

Water is a powerful force. Before you launch, research the area you'll be paddling. Sites such as americanwhitewater.com are supported by kayakers who share their experiences and thoughts on rivers in the area you're interested in. Waterdata.usgs.gov has current information on water conditions in rivers in the area you're interested in. You can also find out online about hazards, rip tides and tidal forces in coastal areas, and other local factors that will affect your time and safety on the water. You don't want to be caught unprepared for a river that's too swift for your skills, or paddling against on out-going tide.

Notes:

Launching

Here's where the fun starts!

Or the humiliation, depending on if you've done your homework and you've practiced what you've read in this chapter.

First make sure that the area you're going to launch from is free of any hazards, and if you're entering a river that the current is slow enough to allow entry into the water safely.

Follow the instructions you found in the "inflation" section, and approach the shore.

Graceful entry takes a certain amount of practice, balance, and athletic ability. Position the kayak parallel to the shore in an inch or two of water (enough so that you won't have to drag the bottom off any potential hazards once you're sitting in the kayak). Place your dominant foot (that's closest to the kayak) inside the cockpit just to the side of center and ahead of the seat while keeping your other foot as close to the kayak as possible. Lean forward, placing your weight on your dominant foot while lifting your other foot inside the cockpit. Grab each side of the cockpit for balance, and slide your feet forward as you lower yourself into the seat. After a little practice you can determine where you need to place your first foot so that when you start to lean back as you move your feet forward you end up in the seat.

If you happen to be like the rest of us, you can stand at the side of the kayak with your back to the cockpit, drop your butt into the seat while spastically swinging your legs high over the side (all in one *smooth* maneuver) and end up in the same position.

This works all right if you don't miss the crucial pivot point and flip the kayak over on top of you. Or if you don't lift your legs too high and flip over the other side, again ending up with the kayak on your head.

Doing it this way may also introduce a gallon or two of very cold water into your seat if you don't flip back and around quickly enough. It's better than coffee to wake you up and get you motivated to paddle and warm up.

Straddling an inflatable kayak can be done, but because of the way it's designed it may prove too difficult for you.

If you have a kayak with a small cockpit you may want to try the method that hardshell paddlers often use. Place your paddle perpendicular to the kayak behind the cockpit. Grab the shaft on either side of center. Sit on the deck behind the cockpit and lift your legs over into the space in front of the seat and slide them forward as you slide into the seat.

Launching into surf requires a different approach. The incoming waves can cause all kinds of problems, so the best way to launch is bow first directly at them. Make sure your kayak is far enough out on the water so that the stern will float off the beach when you push off.

Notes:

Paddling

Next to the quality of the kayak and your PFD, the paddle you choose is the most important piece of equipment you'll use. A kayak may be what keeps you afloat, but a paddle is what moves you through the water – you should put at least as much research into choosing one as you did your kayak.

It should be lightweight, unbreakable (for what you'll be using it for), fit your hands, and be the correct length.

Worst case scenario:

A friend offers the use of one of their kayaks, but without a paddle. You get a decent set of instructions for using the kayak, but you blow off the information about the paddle. How hard can it be?

You finally end up at the Bottom-of-the-Barrel Sports And Beauty Supply Emporium. You find a 9-piece aluminum and plastic paddle for $11.95 at the bottom of a pile of dusty merchandise. The instructions are in a language you don't recognize.

You head down to the river for your first kayaking experience.

You get the kayak to the bank without any problem, but the paddle won't go together despite the threats you make. You have to call for help from a group of slackers, and one guy who's really buzzed just snaps together, and gives you a look. You finally launch with a minimum of splashing, tipping, and more colorful language.

The current catches you, and you instinctively dig the paddle in to avoid the logjam you didn't notice before. The paddle's cheap aluminum tubing kinks and then snaps when you try to use it. The blade that was screwed into the fitting on the other end falls off. You flip sideways, and then under the logjam and get pinned by the current.

All your friends get to see you on the 6 o'clock news, and then one last time in your best suit

As kayaking becomes more popular, there are many more options to choose from for paddles. It used to be that there were very few paddles manufactured, and they all met very demanding standards. Now the choices seem endless, and it can be very confusing to try and determine which one is going to meet your needs.

No matter what paddle you use, the basic rule of thumb is "the lighter the better". It won't matter how you plan to paddle if you can't lift your arms to do it before you're done. Even if you start with short outings, eventually you'll be taking longer and longer trips as you enjoy your kayak more, and the weight of the paddle becomes more important. You can't "grow into" a poor paddle, you can only replace it with a (much) better one.

Research of blade size and shape has led to amazing improvement in paddling efficiency for elite athletes as well as for the rest of us.

Be realistic. Someone of average fitness who tries to use one of the new "super" paddles may look good as they get into their kayak, but the first time they reach forward, dip that super-efficient blade into the water, and give a mighty pull they're going to tear up a muscle or a shoulder, or tip right out into the water.

Especially for a beginner, using a smaller blade will make all the difference in whether it's a good day or not.

Imagine lifting 100 lbs. once versus lifting 10 lbs. ten times or 5 lbs. twenty times. The same principles apply when using a large-bladed paddle versus a smaller-bladed paddle. Using a large blade will exhaust a paddler very quickly, while using a small blade will allow muscle tissue to recover more quickly between strokes, giving the paddler an extended period of time to spend the same energy.

A flat blade is the most "beginner friendly". It moves through the water with moderate resistance, doesn't cause as much "wig-wagging" of the bow, and is very forgiving of inexperienced paddlers. It can be used for long periods of time without inducing severe muscle fatigue.

It may be difficult to find a decent quality paddle with a flat blade. Manufacturers are more than happy to make paddles that are "must-have improvements" over the one you might have now.

A blade with a mild "spoon" may be the best you can do, or it can be your next step up as you become a more experienced paddler.

The least expensive paddles are plastic, come in several pieces, and screw together. You may have occasion to need them if you're flying somewhere and have to save weight and space, and don't plan on doing any paddling other than the absolute minimum in undemanding situations. Always, *always* check the connections for tightness before you leave the shoreline. There's nothing worse (and more embarrassing) than getting out in the middle of a lake or river and have your paddle come apart, then having to watch part of it slowly drift towards the bottom.

Paddles with an aluminum shaft can be inexpensive, and safe to use on a lake. On a river, however, if you put too much stress on the shaft it may kink. The blade may catch on a rock or submerged branch, or you may try to push off an obstacle. An aluminum shaft that has collapsed will be pretty much unusable unless you can snap the shaft in two and use one end to paddle canoe-style.

Paddles with fiberglass shafts and plastic blades can be a great compromise. They can be light, less expensive than carbon-fiber, and much safer to use in a river than aluminum. You can often find them meant for kids with smaller-diameter shafts for their smaller hands and with narrower blades.

The best paddles are made of carbon-fiber. They are extremely light and nearly indestructible, but can be pricey. If you can find one used that hasn't been too abused, you may be able to get a real bargain, and have a paddle that will last you forever.

Paddle blades come in a variety of sizes and shapes, each meant for a different task. Short, wide blades are meant for power (for example, quick maneuvering around river obstacles) while smaller, narrower blades are generally meant for longer distances.

You may notice some blades have grooves molded in to the face. The theory is that the grooves somehow aid the water flow across the face of the paddle. They can make a flimsy paddle much stronger. They're pretty much only found on inexpensive paddles.

Kayak blades generally come in two different shapes – asymmetrical and square. Asymmetrical blades are shaped so that when they enter the water there is an equal area of force above and below the shaft against the water.

A square blade has more area below the waterline than above it, causing the shaft to twist in the paddler's hands. Over a short distance the effect can be negligible, but over any appreciable distance the effect can be severe.

So-called "Greenland" design paddles were developed hundreds of years ago by the Inuits. The blades are long and narrow, developed so that the paddler could travel in shallow water over a rocky bottom without destroying the blade.

Some paddles have "feathered" blades. The blades are set at an angle to each other rather than being on the same plane. If

49

you were to look at a paddle from a distance, if the right blade is vertical, the left blade would be horizontal. Once you get some experience, you may want to experiment with feathering your blades, but for the most part for a novice, you probably won't notice any difference in stroke effectiveness.

It's beyond the scope of this book to teach esoteric paddling techniques. I've tried to provide an easy-to-follow set of instructions to get you started. Simply paddling in a straight line, no matter how wonderful your equipment, will still take practice. Inflatables float on top of the water rather than being in it like hardshells, so they tend to be more affected by wind. Don't think you're going crazy if you're paddling in a crosswind and no matter what you do your kayak always wants to go one way or the other.

Another factor to always keep in mind is weather cocking. The bow is pressing straight against water, and that same water pressure works on either side of the bow to keep the kayak tracking in (sort of) a straight line.

When you stop paddling the pressure is still against the bow, but there are no forces working on the stern. This will cause it to swing to one side or the other, or even in a circle.

Skegs will help minimize the problem. Adding a rudder or anticipating the kayak's action by counter-paddling against the direction the stern is floating can also help.

There are excellent DVD's and on-line videos that can give you much better instruction on more techniques and ways to paddle.

Leaning back and enjoying the sun may be a great way to spend the day, but it won't help you much with basic paddling. Nor will beating the water into submission using only your arms.

The best position for effective paddling is sitting upright, relaxed and with your paddle at shoulder level with your palms about shoulder-width apart, facing away from you. This position will improve your balance, provide the best leverage for delivering power to your stroke, and give you better flexibility and range of motion.

Sitting upright is the most effective way to use the large

muscle groups in your trunk to swivel your torso and leverage smooth power through your arms to your paddle. You need to disconnect your bottom from your upper half so that you can rotate into your paddle stroke with your torso while your butt stabilizes your kayak. You can only do this if you relax and concentrate on a smooth motion. If you tense up, your stomach muscles will be tight and instead of remaining upright you will tilt to one side and then the other with your efforts. Instead of tracking in a straight line you'll be wigwagging all over the place and going nowhere.

There are four basic components of a forward stroke.

First, there is the *reach*. It is very much like it sounds. Extend your right arm and rotate your right shoulder forward, and down, rotating your trunk and reaching forward. This will bring your left shoulder rising up with the left part of the paddle. As you reach relax the outside fingers on that hand. It takes the strain off your wrist and lessens hand fatigue.

Next there is the *catch*. The blade goes into the water up to its base near the bow as you stand the paddle on end. Begin to pull the lower part of the paddle toward you with your right hand. Tighten your hand as the shaft moves toward you.

When you feel it "grab", the *power* phase of the stroke begins. Your left (upper) hand (at about the level of your head) drives forward, your torso twists into the stroke, and your right (lower) hand pulls back towards your hip as your torso finishes it's twist. When it's done right, your right arm should remain straight and your blade should travel in a straight line from your right foot to your right hip.

The *recovery* phase starts when your right blade comes level with your right hip and you start to lift it out of the water with your right hand. The blade should slide out of the water smoothly just behind your hip as your left arm reaches full extension and your left shoulder is rotated forward.

At that point your left hand is in the perfect position to start the stroke on the left side.

It may sound a little complicated, but it's actually pretty simple in practice and becomes a smooth, natural movement very quickly.

Turning requires a *sweep* stroke. To turn, you need to visualize a spin around that imaginary point that would be at the center of a circle around your kayak.

Lean into the direction of the turn, and sweep with your paddle. The farther the blade is from side of the boat, the faster the turn. The closer the blade is to the boat, the more gradual the turn.

It sounds simple, and with a little practice you can be showing off, spinning in circles.

Notes:

Kayaking
and the
Environment

Of all sports, kayaking has one of the lowest impacts on the environment. No green-gas emissions or carbon footprint, no tracks on pristine ground, no trampling of delicate vegetation.

Kayakers tend to be environmentally responsible (who could imagine a bunch of kayakers sitting around and throwing empty beer cans over their shoulders amongst the fast-food wrappers and dirty diapers?).

Sadly, as kayaking becomes more popular, problems with littering, illegal camping, and rude behavior have also become more common. Land that used to be open for considerate kayakers can now be closed to everyone due to inconsiderate behavior. Conflicts between kayakers and other kayakers, power boaters, landowners, law enforcement, and environmental groups caused a severely negative change in the way kayakers are viewed, and it affects us all.

Share boat ramps and other public facilities.

Be familiar with, respect, and adhere to wildlife laws. Just because no one can see you in some remote area doesn't mean you can take advantage and poach or damage the environment.

Respect other kayakers and their equipment. Don't step over, move, or bump into other kayaks (the notable exception is if they haven't secured their kayak and it's starting to float away).

Choose campsites carefully to minimize any impact on the area. You shouldn't have to "make" one, try to find a space that you can use without altering it.

Be very careful with fires, and keep them to a minimum. Remote fires are difficult to contain, and in some areas *any* fire may bring out the vigilantes.

Stick to existing trails. Make every effort to leave no sign of your passing. Litter, human waste, and gray water from dishwashing or bathing needs to be disposed of appropriately, and far away from fresh water.

Respect wildlife. Observe from a distance (at least 100 yards) rather than try to interact with any birds or animals.

Seals, sea lions, orcas, wolves, and bears are all *predators*.

It is relatively easy to silently approach animals in a kayak in an isolated area they've retreated to to escape humans. If startled or protecting their young, they will react. If they feel they are cornered, even the meekest animal will attack. It may seem obvious, but too many people every year are injured or killed by treating them as harmless entertainment.

Don't do it! Besides being dangerous (and stupid), law enforcement can take a pretty dim view of harassing wildlife, and there can be some pretty stiff penalties.

Kayak rescue

Hopefully you'll never have to use the information in this chapter.

Every kayak should have a rope at the bow in case of emergency.

There are generally two types of rescues – those low-intensity everyday events that occur because someone overbalances and ends up in the lake, and the high-intensity OMG disasters that most often happen on rough waters.

Either type is usually the result of one of three things:
Environmental issues
Operator error
Alcohol or drugs

The same applies to lake rescues. Some accidents occur as a result of loss of air (a clumsy fisherman drops a knife, someone gets too close to shore and impales the kayak on a submerged branch), or capsizing with or without a power boat's wake.

Fortunately modern inflatables are almost impossible to sink. In the case of air loss in one chamber a kayaker can usually get to shore or get someone to tow them in.

A capsized inflatable is easy flip over, and getting back in is relatively simple. A strong kick, a reach across the kayak to grab the opposite gunwale, another kick, and a swing of the legs into the boat will usually resolve the problem, especially if you've practiced beforehand.

The river environment, however, can present some severe problems, some of them insurmountable. This chapter is not meant to provide you with all you need to know to enjoy Class V rapids. It is meant to give some practical information and give an overview of the importance of planning, knowledge of the environment, and basic skills.

Practice and preparation can make some of these problems

easy to solve, but we strongly encourage you to find out all you can about local conditions and take classes from professionals before attempting any challenging rivers. An assessment by a professional can give you an accurate appraisal of you skill level and the adequacy of your equipment.

Professionals (or even those who are well-prepared) can make running rapids look easy. Those who are not prepared or up to the task can often be seen on the 6 o'clock news.

Each river has its own unique characteristics that determine how difficult it may be to navigate. Water flow, the geographic makeup of the riverbed, and potential and real hazards all have to be taken into consideration.

Unfortunately, those characteristics can change with water levels and after events like storms. What may be a calm, Class I or II river for some of the year might become something like Class IV after a big storm or heavy snow melt. High flow may uproot trees or move submerged trees to make them formidable obstacles.

Always check water and weather conditions before you start out to make sure you have a safe day.

Notes:

Black River Rescue

We debated whether or not to include this very personal story in this book.
It presents a very graphic picture of what can go wrong very quickly. It demonstrates that "wilderness" doesn't always mean remote, and that help you take for granted may not be there.

Sunday, Black River

We wanted to spend her birthday/our anniversary with a nice, quiet river kayak trip.
If not for Barb, it would have ended with my cold and miserable death.

By all accounts the Black River is a slow, meandering river that runs south and west out of Black Lake south of Olympia. The experts' books describe it as a 5 hour drift with very little current to deal with and almost no bank access. Once you start, you can't get out easily until you reach the downstream SR 12 bridge.

We started out late, just after 4p. Sunset was at 8.30, and we thought if we paddled hard enough we would be able to easily reach the bridge before dark.

The sky was partly cloudy, the temp was 74'. The water was clear and cool, and the trees and underbrush were thick on either bank. We had seen people at the bridge where we would take out, but there was no one where we were putting in. Barb had her camera at the ready, and we launched with a lot of anticipation. What a perfect day.

We hadn't gone very far when we encountered our first challenge, a significant headwind. The air was channeling up between the trees. If we stopped paddling, we would immediately start floating back upstream.

After two wonderful hours we were both beginning to feel the onset of "kayak butt", pain through the hip joints from constantly sitting with your legs pretty much straight out for long periods of time.

We took the first of many breaks out of the wind. At first when we were paddling we didn't talk much. The scenery was spectacular and the day was all we had hoped for.

During our breaks we talked about all kinds of things, things that a couple who had been together nine years and had gone through some challenging times would discuss.

Around 6p. we ran across a couple of guys fishing, and we asked them if they knew how far it was to the bridge.

They looked puzzled and told us they didn't know anything about any bridge, all they had seen was a big sign that essentially said "no access, turn around".

We were just a little dismayed.

We had talked to people at the bridge who had been down the river that day, and eventually decided the fishermen had been having a little fun with us. Great.

So we paddled on. We still had 2 1/2 hours before dusk, we had plenty of time. And no real choice.

It was about 7.30 when we met another boat going upriver. They stopped to chat and we found out they were local. They told us the wind blew upriver pretty much all the time, but the bridge was only about a mile, maybe a mile and a quarter downstream from where we were (we found out later that they had misunderstood, and were talking about a completely different take-out site).

    We figured we had plenty of time to finish, and were looking forward to a nice warm dinner somewhere. We had still only seen one or two houses up through the trees, and there were very few sounds of civilization.

    We think it was an otter that kept pace with us for a little while, maybe hoping we were going to catch a fish he could steal as we reeled it in. After a while he got bored and went his own way.

    A kingfisher stayed with us a little longer, maybe 45 minutes. It would perch ahead of us, dive in the water when we got close, and carry its catch farther downstream and wait for us.

    Towards dusk we started seeing beavers, and were hearing them slap the water with their tails.

    It was maybe 8p. when my seat back collapsed. The side straps holding it up had slipped, and there was no way I could tighten them back up.

I tried paddling without the support, but it was a real

struggle. I'd go maybe 50 or 60 yards, then have to rest, my abdominal and thigh muscles quivering and cramping; the after effects of being paralyzed had caused some weakening of those muscle groups. As soon as I stopped paddling the kayak would spin and the wind would start to move me back upstream. I tried tying up, but all the partially submerged trees along the bank were brittle and snapped easily.

Darkness was beginning to close in. We could see bats flitting above us against the emerging stars, and hear more rustling along the banks. We could hear a large group of coyotes yipping and growling, and another group responding to them.

Sometimes we could hear traffic noises and our hopes would raise that we were finally near the bridge. But then the noises would fade, and so would our hopes.

Barb finally convinced me to let her tow me for a while, and I don't know how much determination it took for her to keep paddling the way she did. I was truly in awe.

We still hadn't seen any sign of the bridge by 9.30p. The sliver of moon had gone behind some clouds, and all we had was faint starlight to navigate by. It was *dark* under those trees. She had tried using the light on her cell phone, but it was just too weak for any helpful illumination, and she wanted to save the battery in case, somehow, we got reception somewhere.

I had talked her into calling 911 earlier, thinking that it was better to be on the 6 o'clock news than to be paddling around in the dark. Surely they had some watercraft for patrolling such a popular river - they could find us and just tow us back to our van at the bridge.

I had no warning when I hit the partially submerged tree. One minute we were quietly floating along, the next I was in the water, in a tangle of branches, next to my upside-down kayak (with the black, slippery hull). My paddle was gone.

After a very short time, my inflatable life vest went off the way it was supposed to. The only problem was, it had snagged on a branch and was up over my ears. My glasses came off (I was somehow able to grab them – a reflex of wearing the damn things for almost 60 years) and the branch I grabbed snapped off. Then another. And a third. I went under again.

I was essentially blind. Without my glasses my world is a blur, anyway, and in the dark all I could see were smudges of dark gray against the black. I was completely disoriented and close to panic.

Barb was able to grab me, and I spent a few minutes in her death grip catching my breath and retching up river water, algae, and probably a beer can or two that someone had thrown in the water. I'm lucky I didn't end up with a plastic bag over my head.

I was able to get an arm over the side of Barb's kayak and hung there in the water. It was too dark to see much of anything, and any time I moved her kayak tipped, so I just dangled there, spluttering and kacking and trying not to capsize her.

During all this Barb had lost her paddle as well, so she couldn't maneuver or even reach for me (or maybe just *accidentally* whack on the head for scaring her so badly).

Somehow she was able to get her cell phone out, and was able to find a weak signal. We found out later that we were in one of the few pockets of service in the area.

She called 911, but had a very difficult time trying to convince the operator how serious our situation was. We didn't *know* exactly where were, *no* we couldn't just climb up on the bank, *no* I couldn't just get in her kayak, *no* Barb couldn't paddle away with me hanging on.

My arm was beginning to cramp, and my thigh muscles were doing the same. I tried moving around, snapped another branch, and went under again. The vest slipped up over my ears again, and this time I had trouble getting my face out of the water under the inflated tubes.

Flailing around, I caught the bow of her kayak, somehow avoiding capsizing her. She was in a panic, thinking she had lost me. As a weak joke (after coughing up another gallon or so of river water, etc. I promised her that I wouldn't die on her birthday.

I just hoped I could keep that promise. I was getting lethargic and losing body heat fast, and beginning to shiver so hard

I was rocking the boat.

I can't say I saw the light at the end of the tunnel, or had any life-changing epiphanies. My life didn't flash before my eyes, but I thought about some of the things I wish I had done, or done differently, and some of the things I wish I hadn't done.

I thought about some of the extraordinary people I had been so lucky to have known, who had inspired me and given me strength: Dr. Lau, the self-effacing genius who had been able to repair some of the heart damage I spent so much time and effort creating; the little boy who, so early in my career, made me promise I wouldn't tell his parents he knew he was going to have life-changing brain surgery, because he didn't want them to worry; Juan, the quietly brave quadriplegic who was facing so much adversity with humor and dignity and helped me face my own paralysis; Dr. Dabb, the best anesthesiologist I'd ever worked with, who would rouse her (always) critically ill patients with her sheer intensity; and Barb, who had stayed with me through so much, always tolerant, supportive, and ready to try stuff like this.

We found out later that 911 did dispatch Fire/Rescue (perhaps because she finally figured out that Barb wasn't kidding, or drunk, or stupid), but they couldn't find us. They didn't have a boat like everyone on TV (not even a bubba they could call on with a bass boat to help out) and they had to search for us on the ground.

We could finally see distant lights through the trees. Barb was talking to Dispatch on the phone, sometimes being terrified when the call dropped and she had to call them back and hope the call would to through.

Barb was yelling so much she was getting hoarse, trying to guide them to us. My whistle could have helped, but it was on my vest, and I couldn't let go to get it.

She kept telling me how sorry she was getting us into this situation, and I kept trying to tell her that it wasn't her fault, and telling her how much I loved her, and reminding her of some of the wonderful times we had spent together.

She kept asking me how I was doing, and I was telling her

I was fine, when I was actually beginning to think about my mortality. I think after a while she was beginning to not believe me. We had, after all, been together for 9 years, she *knew* when I was lying, even when she was letting me get away with it.

The water around me was warmed a little against my skin, but every ripple brought a wave of colder water and more shivering. My arms and hands were cramping, and I was having trouble holding onto the kayak. I caught myself nodding off at times, but Barb always startled me awake.

We could finally hear them thrashing through the underbrush. Dispatch told us that they had had to go through someone's property, and then struggle through the underbrush (including almost impenetrable blackberry bushes with needle-sharp thorns) until they found us.

When they got closer Barb started yelling "Marco!" I'm not sure if they thought she was being funny or delirious.

Suddenly one of them was in the water with me. I must have started thrashing around, but he calmed me down and slowly got me to the bank where they sat me down on a fallen log and wrapped a bunker coat around me (they volunteered the biggest guy there to donate his coat, much to his dismay, I think. Who would want to face the rest of his shift with a coat full of mud and algae?).

They were very professional, much more than I (unfortunately) expected from a rural company. I guess I was flashing back to my days in Prescott when the owner of the other ambulance company would go on runs out of his mortuary by himself (usually without his teeth) and have the neighbors load the unfortunate patient into his Cadillac hearst/station wagon for the perilous ride to the hospital.

I'm afraid I might have seemed just a little ungrateful when, as I sat, I almost got a splintered branch up my butt and maybe a little bit of delirium kicked in ("Please, sir, could you just stop shivering long enough so I can pull these splinters out?" as the whole ER stared and sniggered, and probably took cell phone pictures to post on Facebook). It did motivate me to jump up (where they had to catch me – my left leg weakness had gotten worse) and I finally shifted over a little bit and was able to sit, teetering just a little. I had a fleeting thought that the stress of this would trigger a relapse of all the paralysis, and it scared the crap out of me. Then I got a grip – I had overcome it once, I could do it again if I had to.

They had asked me (maybe just a little bit hopefully) if I felt good enough to walk out, but when they saw me struggling to stand I think they resigned themselves to the drudgery of a rather unpleasant return to their vehicles.

I kept trying to tell bad jokes as I shivered and cramped while they brought a Stokes basket down to carry me out. At the same time they got Barb to shore and kept reassuring her that I was doing OK, but she insisted on seeing for herself.

I heard them discussing what to do with the kayaks, and I told them we would come back in the morning to get them.

I couldn't really see their faces, but the silence was eloquent.

I really didn't want to get into that basket and have them carry my fat ass out, but when I tried to stand my legs locked up and I couldn't keep my balance. Into the basket I went.

I don't know how far they carried me through that jungle, but it was after midnight before they were done.

At one point they even had to slide me across a creek on a 12-inch wide trestle. I know they had to switch off sides and personnel pretty frequently, and by the time we were out of the brush and near the vehicles I could see them all red-faced and sweating.

While they were doing that two of the guys were helping Barb struggle through the same underbrush, and she would occasionally call over (all out of breath) to see if I was still OK.

They transferred me to a stretcher that (thankfully for all of them) had a hydraulic lift to get me into the back of an ambulance with heat lamps and forced hot air.

I told more bad jokes while the paramedic hooked me up and tsk, tsk, tsk'd under his breath. I had warned him how ugly my

EKG was on a good day, but he still got a little pale the first time he looked at it.

He tried to talk me into going to the hospital, and really gave it a great effort. But I had had enough and was finally warming up. I just wanted to go home and sleep. I signed his refusal form, and when Barb arrived with her van (one of them had driven up her up the more than *three miles* to the bridge to get it) I staggered out of the ambulance and, wrapped in a blanket, started to load the kayaks that some of the firemen had actually carried all the way from the river. One of them was apologizing for snagging one of the boats and putting a hole in it. Oh, yeah, *that* seemed important at the time.

They all just kind of stared at the wet, dripping fool who was wrestling the muddy, weed-covered kayaks into the back of the van while trying to hold the blanket together despite all the shivering.

We were able to drive back to my van, me with the heater on "volcano" to warm up and Barb with her head out the window to cool off.

She was very serious when she said, "Well, I guess that's the end of kayaking for us."

"Are you kidding? Of course not! Miss all that fun?"

I think she must have looked at me the same way the rescue team did once or twice.

I convinced her that I was OK to drive, and we started off for home, her following me to make sure I didn't crash or get lost.

We hadn't been on the freeway very long when I saw the signs for a truck stop with a 24 hour McDonalds. I didn't want to admit it, but reaction was setting in and I had to have something hot to eat. Barb wasn't sure I should go inside, but while she got gas I went ahead and staggered in to get us dinner (breakfast? Who cares?) and something hot for me to drink.

I went in with no shirt, still wrapped in that blanket, mud and muck streaking my legs and weeds in my hair. My shorts were still dripping, the water mixing with the blood still running from the scratches and gouges on my legs. I still had the EKG pads on my arms and legs, and I'm sure my lips were still blue.

The kid behind the counter didn't hardly even blink. I told him I had just been pulled out of the river, and he kind of nodded and didn't say anything other than "Dude".

Barb bought me a "Red Neck Rescue" t-shirt over in the truck stop side. It seemed appropriate somehow, and I'll always remember how I was rescued when I wear it. It helps that it is pretty much the same color as all the river mud I had on me (is it possible that she did that on purpose?).

We finally got home at 2.30a. The McDonald's cocoa had given me a buzz (I'm pretty sure he put extra chocolate syrup in it) but I still had some trouble walking into the house. I sure could have used my power chair about then.

The dogs were really excited to see us (we were, after all, 9 hours late for their dinner), but then they got quiet and each one, in turn, came in as I sat on the bed, sniffed my mud-caked shoes and then me, and licked my knee just once to make sure I was all right.

It took me a long time to get to sleep. Besides the cramps and occasional shivering. I couldn't stop thinking about what had happened, and what had almost happened.

Barb had been magnificent, and I was alive because of her.

Chief Scott from West Thurston Fire/Rescue actually called us this morning to follow up and make sure we were OK. Expect *that* from a "modern, professional" service.

He told us how extraordinarily lucky we were, and how difficult it had been to find us. 911 had been able to roughly triangulate us. We had been in one of the few spots that they could actually get to through the forest. They actually sent in two teams to make sure someone got to us as soon as possible. One half mile in either direction and they would not have been able to get to us in time. The water temp was in the 60's, so the time limit was a significant reality.

They had in fact dispatched boats, but like the southern rivers it's been compared to, the Black is so shallow and weed-choked this time of year it's almost impossible to navigate with any boat with a motor. But unlike the southern rivers, there aren't a hundred bubbas around with airboats and a six pack who would absolutely salivate for a *legal* excuse to blast down the river in the middle of the night at full speed.

The only helicopters available were 1) a Coast Guard bird from the coast with a response time measured in hours (if they didn't have a sea-related rescue to attend to first) and 2) a medical chopper without the capabilities to winch me out.

He also told us they had been inundated by calls from the press, wanting more details, especially our full names (they have access to the 911 tapes, but not the service reports). There's a short story in the Centralia Chronicle, and we're taping the local news channels to see what they have to say. One channel has requested an on-camera interview. Repeatedly.

I readily admit to not being impressively photogenic, and I certainly don't want *everyone* to know how stupid I've been.

On the other hand............. fame is calling me.

Film at 11!

Accessories

There are always things to add and ways to improve your kayak and your experience on the water:

Waterproof camera
Nothing is more fun than boring everyone you know with pictures! Pictures can also document your progress as a paddler, along with all the mishaps of your partner, kids, and anyone you've been able to convince, cajole, or blackmail into going with you.

Waterproof Case
Essential for protecting electronic car keys (that won't work if submerged!), phone, camera (if you don't have a waterproof one), and anything else you don't want to get soaked.

Quality Hat
There is a reason for those dorky-looking hats. The cool-max like materials (or gore-tex) keep your head cool and protect you from the sun. The wide brim keeps water from your paddle from running down your neck into your shirt. If it rains, it keeps your face dry. And, of course, makes you look like a real kayaker dude.

Quality Sunglasses
Polarized sunglasses allow you to see below the water surface, and cuts the glare off the water. UV protection limits damage to your eyes from ultraviolet radiation. Lenses that are not distorted will keep your eyes from being fatigued and causing headaches that can be a real problem after a long day on the water while you're still far from done.

Paddle

You can never have a good enough paddle. And if you ever find the perfect paddle for one kind of kayaking, you still need to find the perfect one for other kinds of paddling. The science of paddle design is rapidly growing. As the sport of kayaking grows, so does the demand for better equipment and better performance.

Seat

The same basic inflatable seats have been around since Sevylor built that first kayak. Since then there has been some improvement as far as inflatable seat design goes, but much more progress has been made in adapting non-inflatable seats to inflatable craft.

Many manufacturers now have added D-rings to their kayaks so that seats can be attached securely and comfortably for the paddler. Some manufacturers provide only minimal seating with poor or no back support. These are the same "old school" guys who believe that kayaks should only be made for people weigh about 100 lbs. And can paddle for days at a time, subsisting on power bars and roots and berries.

Be comfortable! There are some minimal inflatable seats that may be adequate for you. They don't attach to anything but can be moved easily and double as a camp chair. They rely on a separate air chamber for back support.

They're usually not very comfortable for long trips, but they're easily repositioned to fit individual paddlers.

Sea Eagle has a seat that can be free-standing (and used as a camp chair) or can be clipped into a kayak for a little more security.

The higher back and side straps provide a little more back support.

For any kind of spirited paddling you need a seat that is secured and supportive. They usually clip in to D-rings or some other structure attached to the hull of the kayak, but are limited in fore-and-aft adjustment.

Handles

Handles are a great thing to have. Inflatables can be awkward to manage. They're large and slippery when wet, and can act like a kite when there's wind blowing.

D-rings

If you're going to carry any gear that you don't want floating away in a mishap, or moving around, D-rings (or grommets) are a great way to secure it.

Several manufacturers now offer D-rings in a variety of sizes and materials for watercraft made with different materials. You can make your own and incorporate velcro to make it even more useful.

In lieu of metal rings, if you have a fabric-covered kayak with separate air bladders you can sew narrow canvas webbing into loops in several different areas. Just be sure to protect the inner bladder from puncture.

They can be unobtrusive, non-abrasive, and very handy.

Boxes, bags

There is nothing you will need more than whatever it is you left behind.

There are any number soft and hard tackle boxes and gear bags available that, if you are so inclined, can not only meet your needs but also color-match your kayak.

They can be secured in several ways. If you have

deck rigging, you can tuck the bag under the cord if it's small

enough. You can use industrial-strength velcro to keep the bag secure.

　　　If you're a fisherman and need easy access to your tackle, you can attach bags to each   side tube within easy reach.
　　　Cooler

You should always carry some kind of fluids with you. You can also see in this picture a small cooler placed behind the seat. It's normally secured to the kayak's cargo clip (it's always better to have coolers with attached lids, especially if you're on a river). A "soft" cooler rather than a hard plastic cooler may be easier to fit into the inner contours of a narrow kayak.

Foam paddle grips (in attractive colors)
If you'd like to be color-coordinated or just plain fashionable, you can get foam paddle grips in different colors. If your hands are big enough, these can make long trips more comfortable.

Thigh pads
You usually wouldn't need these unless you were doing some pretty spirited paddling in fast or turbulent water. The pads work to help your lower body stay secure in the kayak and allow you to pitch your weight if necessary.

Paddle leash
Usually necessary only for fast water, a paddle leash will keep you from losing your paddle. The downside is that if you lose your paddle and it becomes trapped, the leash may remain attached and pull you out of your kayak.

Compass
Hopefully you would never need one. If you were on a long trip or on a large body of water you might need one.

GPS
Probably more useful than a compass if you were on a large body of water or on a river in a wilderness and needed to know exactly where you were. It can also pinpoint put-in and take-out sites.

Whistle

You may need a whistle if you or someone you are with need to communicate or call for help. Every person in your group (including kids!) should have one attached to their PFD.

Anchor

Remember that inflatables are at the mercy of wind and waves. If you're doing anything that you would want to remain in one place for (fishing, birding, photography) you need something to hold you there.

Sun Shade

The sun can be brutal out on the water. If you are going to spend a lot of time out there (and especially if you burn easily) Windpaddle sells an excellent bimini top (along with sails). Or you might want to investigate several excellent videos on the Internet for fabricating a simple sun shade for you kayak.

Bling

There is an astonishing number of decals, bumper stickers, t-shirts, keychains, necklaces and other jewelry, and even antenna toppers to show your interest in kayaking.

Notes:

Repair

An inflatable kayak is a fairly simple craft, with few moving parts. The materials it's made of and its construction determine its durability. Your actions as its paddler will determine how long it remains useable.

If you have the perfect kayak (for you) that you want to enjoy forever and want to be preemptive, there is something you can do to protect it. It's a little pricey ($53/quart at this writing) but may be worth it over the long run. It's called toobseal, and you just pour it into your air chambers. It coats the inside walls and forms a second layer of protection against leaks.

The reality is that if you own an inflatable, at some time you will need to repair it. *Always* carry a repair kit with you. It should consist of a spare valve (if you have Bostons), several pre-cut patches, glue, single packs of alcohol pads (to clean the area to be patched), and q-tips. There are quick-repair tear off strips on the market, but I've never used them and can't say if they're effective. I've heard of duct tape being useful (hasn't everybody?) but I would discourage its use. Cleaning up the adhesive from the tape after you get home can be tiresome. If you take care of your kayak, though, it can give you years of pleasure. (Note: as a general rule of thumb, bad things tend to happen within 5 feet of the waterline).

As I mentioned previously, I have a Sea Eagle 340 that was manufactured in 1979 and is still as safe to use today as it was then

on local lakes, bays, and Class II - III rivers.

I also own a less expensive boat made of a single thickness of PVC that I would consider only safe for lakes, and it probably won't last nearly as long as the 340, no matter how careful we are with it.

There are 3 natural enemies of inflatable kayaks:
1. objects sharp enough to put a hole in an air bladder
2. sunlight/UV light
3. operator error

The material the kayak is made of has a direct affect on resistance to puncture. Some kayaks are made of a single thickness of PVC, and are the most susceptible to punctures, rips, and tears.

Some manufacturers encase the PVC air bladders in layers

of material to minimize the risk of punctures. Others may use a single layer of a combination of materials such as PVC, nylon, and polyester (and, in some cases, even Kevlar) to make them extremely tough.

Whatever your kayak is made of, if you have a structural failure and the craft is still under warranty, contact the manufacturer as soon as possible. Keep your descriptions short and succinct, and send photographs. Lots of photographs. Be aware that some companies are much more customer-friendly than others, and be prepared for some resistance. If you experience immediate and amazing service, tell your friends!

No matter what the kayak is made of, sunlight will cause significant deterioration. One of the biggest complaints in customer reviews involves a kayak "disintegrating" after it's been left out in the sun constantly (i.e. on the deck of a sailboat). With just a little care to protect that boat (i.e. put it inside or cover it up when the sailboat was docked) that kayak would have lasted years longer.

Leaks are an inevitable part of life with an inflatable, and there are any number of reasons for them. Over inflation is probably the number one cause. I can't stress enough that you need to follow the manufacturer's guidelines closely. If in doubt, inflate until the air chamber is firm but can be depressed with moderate finger pressure (approximately one atmosphere). Pressure gauges are available and must be used on high-pressure craft to ensure optimum performance (these craft may be designed for pressures of two or three atmospheres).

As the day warms up the air in the chambers will expand and increase the pressure even if the boat's in the water, so periodically check for high pressure. Never leave a fully inflated craft unattended out in the sun. The next sound you may hear is your kayak exploding.

Never allow anyone to sit, step, or place equipment on your kayak unless it's in the water. Even a small child can cause at least a pinhole if you're not careful. You may have to start your day repairing a leak rather than enjoying the water. Or worse, interrupt your day to paddle like mad for the shore to get there before your leaking air chamber collapses.

You can do many small repairs yourself. They can be simple and successful if you follow the directions and keep a few things in mind.

If possible, do repairs when the humidity is under 70%. Higher than that, the adhesive won't dry thoroughly and the bond strength won't be very high. (Although one product, Vyna-bond, claims it can be applied successfully underwater).

Try to avoid any repairs while the temperature is above about 78 degrees. Heat will cause the adhesive to cure unevenly, affecting the bond strength. Working in direct sunlight will have much the same effect.

Ideally, you should work inside in a controlled, well-ventilated environment. Glue and vapors are very flammable, so avoid any smoking or open flame (i.e. if you want to work in a garage or basement, make sure there's not an open flame for the furnace or water heater). If the fumes are concentrated enough, even a spark from static electricity or a light switch can ignite them

To find the source of a slow leak in a kayak (especially with Adams valves or Boston valves), first inflate to the appropriate pressure and listen closely to the valve for air leaking. One good way to tell if it's a valve is to be sure to snug down the cap tightly and see if that seems to slow the leak. If it's a Boston valve that's leaking (most often caused by inflating with a high-pressure hose, like at a gas station) it can be easily replaced. The thin diaphragm at the base of the valve is easily damaged and cannot be replaced or repaired. You can quickly check if dirt or debris is keeping the diaphragm from sealing. If that's the case, wash it gently with a mild soapy solution if you can and see if it still leaks. If it does, replace it from the repair kit you should carry with you at all times.

Plano and other manufacturers now make several sizes of watertight containers that come with their own clip to attach to your kayak that will hold a repair kit. You can also try using a large semi-rigid sunglasses case that will hold everything and use a carabineer to attach it securely.

There are two most common sizes of Boston valves (and at least three more that you will rarely see), and usually you have to buy a package with one of each size in it. You'll have to try each valve to figure out which one fits your kayak.

AirHead has a package with a green cap included that will accept air from a gas station hose or a compressor without blowing out the valve.

Sevylor sells a kit with valves, adhesive and clear patch material, and odd pieces that can be quite handy.

If you have the bad luck to have a leaky Adams valve, you will have to take it to a professional shop and have the whole valve replaced. The valve will have to be cut out and replaced with whatever type of valve you choose and enough fabric to ensure that the valve will be secure.

To find a pinhole, you can start by inflating the kayak and listening for the air leak. Use soapy water either sprayed on or sponged on one area at a time and look for bubbles. Be patient! It may take some time. If you get frustrated or try to hurry, stop and return to it another time. If you've spent hours without finding the leak and you have Boston valves, you can squirt a small amount of water into the air tube, inflate it, and watch for drops of water leaking from the tube. Be sure to empty the water out afterwards.

Once you've found the pinhole, mark it. There are several types of glue on the market specific for the different materials most popularly used. (For simplicity, I'll describe what's necessary for PVC, but the same principals apply to other materials).

The best results occur if you can get glue on both sides of the hole. Clean and dry the area. Inflate the kayak and let the escaping air dry out the inside of the hole. Use alcohol or some other mild solvent (NOT toluene!) to remove any old glue or contaminants. Put a small amount of glue on an applicator of some kind (a toothpick works well) that is smaller than the hole. Fold the material so that the hole is at the top of the fold and insert the glue, applying it to the inside of the tube. Let it flatten and apply glue to the outside of the hole and to an area around it to assure good adhesion.

Let the glue dry according to the instructions on the package, then apply another layer of glue. Allow it to dry overnight, then inflate the kayak and apply different types of pressure to the area to make sure the leak is sealed and secure.

For larger punctures, patch kits are available from some manufacturers to match the color of the kayak.

You may need to think outside the box if none of these are available. We don't recommend it, but on a camping trip some friends of ours got a rather large hole in their boat. He ended up cutting a hole out of their inflatable (PVC) mattress, glued it over the puncture, and they managed to get home with this huge freckle on the side of their kayak (and an interesting story).

To repair a large hole, the same environmental rules apply. Clean the area thoroughly. If the hole is large enough, to ensure the integrity of the patch slip a piece of patch material into the hole that is 1/4" larger than its opening. You may have to glue a small piece of plastic or a rubber band to the center of the patch to protrude out of the hole so you can pull the patch against the inside of the wall. Center it inside the hole and apply a thin layer of glue with a small applicator around the perimeter of the patch. Apply pressure to squeeze out any air bubbles. Apply a weight to the area and allow it to cure for at least 12 hours.

Next prepare a patch at least 1/2" larger than the hole. Cut off whatever you used to pull the interior patch against the hull, and apply a thin layer of glue completely covering the area to be repaired and to the surface of the patch. Apply the patch, making sure to squeeze out any air bubbles. After 10 minutes the glue should be tacky enough to remain sealed without any more air bubbles forming. Apply a weight and allow to sit for 12 hours. Inflate to pressure and use soapy water to check for any air leaks.

If there are any air leaks around the perimeter of the patch, clean and dry the area again, seal with glue, allow 12 hours to cure, and check again.

Seam repairs can be a challenge. Several companies sell

"seam sealer" that may work on smaller problems (as long as the seam is not separated). If the seam is sewn and intact but leaking through the thread holes, Coghlan's makes a seam sealer for nylon and synthetics with a nozzle that can get you into tight spots. Regular patch glue, while essentially the same stuff, is too thick to run down into the smallest crevices and thread holes. Retailers like Amazon sell plastic "welders" that, with practice, can be used to repair all kinds of damage or replace valves, add D-rings, etc.

If you decide to try a seam repair yourself, follow the steps above and be sure to not only inflate the air chamber when you're done but also test it for flexibility. Keep it inflated for a while to see if the repair holds up.

Most seam repairs require professional attention. Check with your kayak's manufacturer for local sources or advice on how to achieve the safest repairs.

Notes:

More notes:

Maintenance and Storage

Okay, now that you've had a wonderful time with your kayak, you need to put it away clean, dry, and protected.

Every time you use your kayak you need to at least wash it to get all the gunk and pollution off of it. It may not show up until later, but even the cleanest looking water can have pollutants in it that may not hurt your kayak, but may stain it.

If you're going to really treat your kayak well, washing it with a mild detergent and then rinsing it well is best. At the end of the season an application of preservative/UV protectant will keep it's material supple so you won't be greeted with any cracks when you unfold it the next spring as you get ready for enjoying it for another summer.

Take the time to let your boat dry. With modern materials a kayak that is stored wet may not rot, but it will mildew. The next time you take it out it will look like it's been ravaged by some dread disease. If you're really unlucky, you may get some multicolored mold, as well.

There are some who suggest keeping your kayak partially inflated to avoid creases in the material that form when it's stored in one position for long periods of time. In a perfect world you would have the space to keep your kayak inflated all winter, but in reality keeping it inflated negates one of the reasons (limited space) you may have had for buying an inflatable in the first place.

Material that has been treated with a protectant will remain supple and easy to fold and squeeze into your storage bag. Creases that form will not become permanent under most conditions. Examine the material closely. Are cracks beginning to form in certain areas? All the more reason to apply liberal quantities of protectant. Rub it in to the material to avoid any more damage and your kayak will be able to stay with you for a long time.

You can protect your kayak while storing it by using a storage bag, duffel bag, or even a suitcase to keep it from any harm. The material should be heavy enough to protect your kayak from any inadvertent contact with sharp objects or edges, but not airtight so any moisture may escape. Military surplus stores have all kinds of storage bags that may meet your needs (the Flyer's Kit Bag is great for any of the smaller kayaks). Manufacturers and outfitters have storage bags, but they tend to be pricey.

It seems to be a universal law that no matter what you get for storage, it's going to be 1" too small, and you'll spend hours trying to squeeze your boat into it. Things will go much better if the kayak is warm and pliable (that's how the factory got the damn thing in there in the first place).

No matter how you pummel, press, or swear, there will always be air left in the bladders. You can empty them more thoroughly by attaching the air filler hose to the "deflate" side of your pump and sucking the last of the air out.

Then you can either roll up your kayak or fold it. If you lay it flat, bottom down, fold the sides inward, then the point of the bow to mid-kayak. Fold the point of the stern over until it touches the point of the bow, then fold the whole thing over again. You'll have a compact package with the bottom out at all sides, protecting the inside of the kayak.

This is especially important if the bottom of the kayak is made of tougher material than the top, and if you have skegs or strakes – the harder material will be resting against the tough part of the hull, not the inside of the kayak.

The storage bag will also make it easier to carry your kayak and keep it from harm while you're transporting it to and from your destinations.

You should store your kayak out of the way, in an area without any severe temperature extremes and out of reach of any critters that may find it irresistible.

Notes:

More notes:

Kids and kayaking

Kids take a particular joy in kayaking. They can scoot across the water, exploring their independence. And, of course, they can make great splashes with their paddles, soaking everyone.

When you're sharing quality time with your child, try not to be The Grownup. Share in *their* version of fun (while keeping the Adult With the Rules at bay, except in life-threatening situations).

Children as young as two (if they're potty-trained) can enjoy paddling (either as an observer or active participant). It's up to you to determine their abilities and needs (some youngsters are eager to explore everything, some need a full-time keeper).

Kayaking can provide kids with that little something that adds to their stature among their peers, and to their confidence.

Talk to your kids about how they feel about going out on

the water. We were taken aback when we took our 8 year old nephew out for the first time and he got really upset. He had heard stories about kids drowning in the lakes and he was afraid it was going to happen to him. He had been out on motorized boats for years without any problems, but he was very specific about the inflatables. We had no idea about his fears and it took some effort to actually get him started paddling. Once he did he had a great time, but it could have been a very difficult day.

The first thing you need to do when you start to seriously think about getting kayaks is to introduce your kids to safety concepts. The sooner they learn about safety and respecting the water they'll be around, the less you have to worry and the safer they'll be. (Of course, once they learn all the safety rules they'll start lecturing you on what you're not doing right, but that's a discussion for another day).

The Coast Guard offers boating safety classes, and your Red Cross, YMCA, and outfitters' stores like Cabela's and Bass Pro Shops can often tell you where classes are available.

Go to the classes together. It may open a few doors for some meaningful conversation and (as corny as it may sound) a way for you to express to them how much you care about their safety.

Kids should be able to swim before they go out on the water. The unexpected always happens, and it's a small thing that may mean everything in a disaster.

Each child should have a life vest that fits snugly but is not binding. Stay away from those ugly orange things that have the two parts in front connected to the piece that goes behind the neck. They're clumsy and uncomfortable, and your day may be ruined if your kid is unhappy and vocalizes all day the way only a child can. Sporting goods stores (or even your local Goodwill) will have inexpensive vests that will fit your kid for a season or two, and would be well worth the cost. Just make sure they haven't been abused or altered, and fit your child well.

An appropriate-sized paddle is also important. Kids need an almost-adult sized paddle, not a short one that you'll have to throw away and replace anyway. 200 – 210 in an inflatable is just about right.

Your first excursion on the water should be as non-threatening as possible. Keep it low-key and do what you can to minimize any anxiety. Stay away from fast or turbulent water. Even if they seem all right, kids can feel a lot of anxiety that will affect their enjoyment, and yours.

Take a camera and try to unobtrusively take candid pictures as well as using it to encourage them to do what you need them to do.

Think of new things to look for and explore. On a lake, maybe an island. On a river, there's all kinds of wildlife to capture a child's interest and imagination.

Choose an area away from kamikaze bugs. Bug spray is noxious, swatting all the time is distracting and annoying, and the itching later will be remembered forever.

Make sure the child knows what you expect of him or her. You can involve them in the preparation for the day. If you think your child is capable, give him or her a checklist and put the child in charge of making sure everything on the list makes it to the car (just make sure you discreetly double check).

Make a plan for the day and let your child know what is

expected of him/her, what you all will be doing, and when. You can head off any resistance early, and maybe get some suggestions for fun that you hadn't considered. Make sure the plans match the child's attention span. A bored kid means misery for everyone.

I know it sounds over-simplistic, but have enough adults to make sure no kids get away when they start feeling adventurous. You won't hear them leave, and they can slip away pretty easily if you have a boisterous crowd.

Paddling by itself may not hold the interest of some kids, who may be more interested in swimming. One new model that's a very stable sit-on-top and light enough for kids to paddle is the Rogue from Aquaglide:

It's stable enough to act as a swimming/snorkeling platform and inexpensive enough to invest in until they either progress to better kayaks or decide they'd rather not paddle.

Take plenty of water (NOT sports drinks) to avoid any problems with dehydration. Keep most of them in the freezer until the last minute so that they can thaw throughout the day, providing cold water in the hottest part of the day. Be sure you don't leave the empty bottles anywhere. Always carry out what you carry in.

Try not to take any hand-held games. I guarantee they'll end up at the bottom of the lake, and you *know* what happens next.

Plan on rest stops. Especially on a longer trip, kids can get tired pretty easily. You may be able to arrange some space in your kayak for them to take a nap if you're in a tandem, or you may plan to tow them if they're in their own boat.

Have plenty of towels and warm, dry clothes ready when you're done for the day to avoid any problems with hypothermia. If you have the means, it may be a good idea to have hot drinks or soup ready, as well.

At then end of the day you might have a pin or a patch your kid can keep and wear to commemorate a successful day.

Notes:

Clear Kayaking

This one of those specialized topics that doesn't really fit anywhere else, with a very specialized purpose.

Some manufactures (Sevylor, Dyad) have made clear windows in the floor of their kayaks for years, to aid in the exploration of the waters below their kayaks. They're most popular around tropical reefs where colorful wildlife abound, and are very good at captivating the interest of kids – no matter what their age.

Clear Blue Hawaii has gone one step further – they have started making kayaks that are completely transparent.

The "skin" is a polycarbonate material stretched over a 6061 aluminum frame (the same material many mountain bikes are made of). It provides almost complete visualization of its environment (obstructed only by frame, seats, and gear).

We can't think of a better way to spend a vacation than paddling in crystal clear water and being able to see below.

It sounds like a great concept, and a wonderful way to explore the marine environment without disrupting it.

Unfortunately, we've not been able to find any objective evaluations of the kayaks' characteristics, durability, or quality. There isn't even enough information to hazard any educated guesses.

If you want to use one of these during a tropical vacation, we suggest renting at your destination rather than buying.

Previous efforts at "windows" have been successful – until the plastic is permanently scratched. Damage has occurred by dragging the kayak across the shore or over obstructions, inappropriate shoes, and sharp-edged gear.

If this new polycarbonate material is, indeed, impervious to such damage and the construction and design of these kayaks is equal to their costs, the opportunity exists for an unforgettable experience.

Kayleighn's Story

When I was nine my grandparents started talking about taking me with them when they went kayaking.

I was pretty excited. I had this picture in my head about kayaking. I had seen pictures on TV with these guys out at sea, doing this great paddling, and other guys going down these rapids.

I thought it would be pretty cool to be able to paddle across this smooth water, and be able to tell my friends about stuff they couldn't do.

At the same time, I was a little scared. I could swim OK, but I had never thought about kayaking, and I didn't have any idea if I would be any good at it. I don't play a lot of sports, and I was afraid I wouldn't be able to do it very well. Was I going to tip over as soon as I got in it? Could I even get that vest on without getting all tangled up in the straps? Was I going to drop the paddle? Or paddle wrong? The more I thought about it, the more scared I got that I'd look stupid and everyone would laugh at me.

One day we all crammed into my grandparents' "Boat-mobile" and we drove to this lake way out in the woods. It was pretty, and not very big. I tried not to be scared, and my grandfather kept telling stupid jokes and stuff while they got things ready. I guess it helped a little.

Everyone was running around and being busy when my little sister grabbed the best small kayak and took off with it. So instead I got this red blow-up kayak that my sister was supposed to get that seemed a little cheap.

Grandpa had put a floor in it, but when I got in it the stupid thing folded up like a taco because I was too big. I tried paddling it, but the "kids" paddle was too short and it was just too hard. And nobody told me I was going to be sitting in cold water! I felt pretty stupid out there in front of everybody, but no one really laughed at me.

They finally towed me back to shore and Grandpa got out another kayak that was a *lot* better. I could sit up in it, and the paddle was long enough that I didn't have to lean over all the time. I could paddle it fine, and it was fun to go out on the lake. Now I imagine I look like some of those guys in the video (but not the ones going down the rapids).

I've got my own kayak, vest, and paddle now, and I've gotten very good at paddling. It's a lot easier, too. My new boat glides across the water, and can turn very quickly, too. I'm going to decorate it and my vest a little to make them look cool. I'll bet I'm the only girl out kayaking.

I'm twelve this summer, and we're going to go down some rivers. I can't wait! Kayaking is a lot more fun now.

Barb's Story

This was written by my fiancé, and he's convinced me to include it against my better judgment. The names have not been changed to protect the innocent

Paddle Faster! I Hear Banjo Music!!   8/07

Craigslist ad:
Wanted: congenial folks with a sense of humor to share kayak adventures. No athleticism required. Lifeguard experience a plus.

You know, when you're upside down in the water, trying not to suck in any fish, muck, weeds, or trash, it is difficult to remember how to do that "Eskimo roll" thing that that smug bastard was trying to teaching us in the class.

One day after Roger and I spent some time rowing erratically around the lake and Rene and Barb sat on the bank laughing at us, Barb told me again (wistfully) about her dream to kayak (actually, she said "I would LOVE to be able to………." and, being trainable, I leaped into action). Her birthday was coming up, so I started looking around for something that I thought she would like.

It was fairly easy to find something suitable (as opposed to that OTHER inflatable kayak with all the holes in it) by researching on line, but I decided that I needed some personal interaction.

Have you ever been in one of those fancy places? It's like a church! I didn't mind being ignored so that they wouldn't see the shock on my face when I saw the prices. $30 for a "rock-climber's" keychain? How is a *keychain* going to help me climb a pile of rocks? (other than lightening my wallet, of course). And if I pay $200 for a pair of pants that haven't been signed by a pro basketball player, I want them to do more than drape fashionably.

Unfortunately, the person I encountered most often was either the taciturn weather-beaten guy half my weight ("OK, I'll indulge you until something more important comes up, like hugging a tree") or the 20-something who looked at me like I was *old* (and delusional). I hope the skateboard I crushed in the parking lot was the one he rides to work every day.

So I tried calling around instead. How can you sneer over the phone? "You need to *ask*." and "I don't really know anything about local water – I'm an *ocean* kayaker".

Oh, well. I decided to spend some effort on accessorizing her gift with safety equipment instead:

Emergency flotation device: I glued a rubber ducky to the top of her hat.

Emergency locater: a compass so she can tell which way she's (not) going.

Emergency signal (besides screaming): big orange whistle (birds fell out of the trees when she tried it out at home)

Emergency alert: miniature radio with weather updates in case a hurricane (or blizzard, tsunami, tornado, cyclone, wind shear, etc.) comes in while she's out on the water.

Emergency remote inflator: O2 mask with tubing – not only can it be used to inflate in the case of unfortunate deflation, but cures hyperventilation as well!

Emergency beacon: magnifying glass so she can start a signal (forest) fire if she gets lost.

Emergency communicator: walkie-talkie. (Shouting into the thing) "Where am I? I'M RIGHT OUT HERE, YOU IDIOT!!!!!"

And, under "misc", is the kayaker antenna-topper and a motivational t-shirt ("Paddle harder! I hear banjo music!").

Yesterday was the perfect day for a bucolic afternoon of paddling, so we loaded up and went down to the Humptulip River (seriously, I can't make this stuff up). She had the kayak I had found for her on craigslist (>$200) and mine was the one I had found at St. Vincent DePaul (<$5).

Did I mention it was late September in western Washington?

So, we get down to the water, and as the more experienced boater I step into the water (and break the ice) and warn her that the ramp is may be slippery.

I, of course, slip and cartwheel down the slope, flailing and snorting and sputtering. Did I mention it was late September?

Now my nose is dripping and my eyes are streaming. My ears are sloshing and I don't think I'll ever find my ****** again. Gobbets and strings of algae and weeds are in my hair and eyebrows and hanging from my glasses and from inside my nose. And I get a 3.2 from the East German judge.

The walkie-talkie in my shirt pocket shorts out, sending a huge jolt through my left nipple (this from a radio that won't broadcast to the end of the block). My left arm shoots out straight, sending the kayak up in the air where the wind catches it. It sails into a boat coming in. It smacks the driver in the face before he can duck, turning the boat right into the dock. The backwash from the boat knocks me over backwards into the water again. My foot is suddenly cold.

Did I mention it was late September?

Things finally settle down, I get the kayak back, and notice my shoe, just out of reach, sinking out of sight.

As soon as she can stop laughing enough to get her breath I put my kayak on the dock and help Barb get into hers. No problem. She slips into it like a pro and paddles off

She gets a 3.*3* from the East German judge. How unfair is *that*?

So I get mine, line it up against the dock so I can get in it gracefully without it skating out from under me, and as I get in the air valve lip catches on the edge of the dock, flipping it up. There's a sudden a piercing whistle of escaping air as the boat collapses around me. My foot slips across and over the other side, my toes whack the dock (the white flash of pain causing my leg to spasm), and suddenly the boat's caught between my knees while both ends flip up around my head. I can't see, I can't reach around it, I'm hopping around on one foot (the other one is too tender), and I finally bounce against the dock and flop into the water. The walkie-talkie gives me another jolt, and this time my arm flies up and I hit myself in the head.

I throw the radio in disgust, there's a flash of light, and three trout float to the surface. The dockmaster/game warden comes over shaking his head, and I know I'm in trouble. He looks at me with the weeds and algae hanging off me as I hold this flaccid boat, and tells me I have enough trouble. He scoops up the fish in a net.

I blow the kayak back up and try to get in it without getting near the dock. I hoist my leg into the cockpit and it flips over with my leg caught under it. I finally get my head above water again, and try getting near the dock. The valve pops open again. I blow it up again, and try turning it around against the dock so the valve is on the opposite side. I barely get my leg over the gunwale and about a gallon of water gets in with me. I end up face down with one leg bent over my butt and the other one trapped under the deck again. I squirm around to get face up, the kayak tipping ominously, and I'm beating the water to a froth as I flounder around. I eventually get to where I'm sitting up where I'm supposed to be, breathing hard enough to almost drown out the noises Barb is making.

I float away from the dock feeling smug despite being

soaked and not being able to see through my glasses. Then I realize my paddle is still on the dock. I can see the dockmaster pondering whether he should hand it to me or save himself a search-and-rescue effort later.

We paddle around for a couple of hours, peaceful and quiet. I only whine a little through chattering teeth. Barb tells me she has water in her cockpit as well, trying to make me feel better.

We finally get back to the dock, and the dockmaster looks thunderstruck. And relieved.

Barb gets out first, tips her kayak, and about a tablespoon of water dribbles out. I try to get out and just flop over the side. Right then there's a tsunami wave from a passing boat that knocks me over face first in the water. Three people come over to try and lift me onto the deck, one piece at a time. I finally get upright, tilt my boat, and about 3 more gallons of water and a frantic perch fall out.

For the next hour I carry stuff from the dock to the van, lurching along with one shoe squishing with each step. I can't feel my feet.

On the way home I'm on auto-pilot and without thinking I pull into the drive-through at the Hot Chick a Latte to get something hot enough to stop my teeth from chattering.

Barb says "Have you ever been here before?"

Oops.

"Oh, NOO-OO-OO, it's just the nearest place to get something to drink."

This scantily-clad sweet young thing waves and, smiling widely, leans w-a-a-a-a-a-a-y out of the window into the cold wind, nearly knocking over her tips jar crammed with cash. She calls me by name, and asks if the dogs are with me this time.

I, of course, glance at Barb to see if she noticed. Duh.
What was I THINKING???
Oh, yeah.
Did I mention it was September?

Disabled Kayaking

Note: My fiancé was hit with a nasty little paralyzing syndrome called Giullian-Barre. He was told that the best he could hope for was to maybe learn to feed himself, but it would take extensive therapy. Happily, that turned out not to be the case.

For most people with disabilities the inherent stability of the inflatable kayak can provide a safe and exhilarating way to enjoy the water.

The major obstacle facing someone with disabilities is access to the kayak's cockpit. The side tubes of an inflatable are usually large, and the paddler sits down between them. Getting over the tube and down into the boat may be easier than getting up and out over the same tube.

Once you're there, for a time the frustration of limitations are forgotten.

Getting Prepared

The first step in the process is a complete and objective assessment of the person's abilities and limitations. The health care team, with the help of an experienced kayaker, should determine if the person will be able to safely participate in what kinds of activity.

An appropriate kayak has open access to the cockpit, even though that exposes the paddler to the elements. Someone who may be adversely affected by heat or cold should determine what weather and water conditions are best before starting out.

Conditioning

Emphasis should be placed on exercises involving balance and upper body strength, shoulder mobility, and the use of trunk muscles to aid in paddling.

The Kayak

There are many things to consider when choosing an appropriate craft. For some with severe mobility issues, a hardshell sit-on-top was the only answer to kayaking of any time. Now, there are several inflatable alternatives.

Some models have smaller side tubes that are easier to get over. Others have either a flat deck, or a shallow cockpit and a flat deck.

A new model from Aquaglide combines the two best features:

It has a shallow well to sit in with pontoons to add stability. It may not be as rigid or as durable as some of the other kayaks, but it's much less expensive, and should be durable enough for casual paddling.

Some models, like Sea Eagle, have large air chambers, so that someone who has balance issues may feel more comfortable.

However, side pontoons and a fairly deep cockpit may make it difficult for some to get in and out of these.

Companies like Airis and Maxxon make excellent sit-on-tops with a shallow well that are rigid (better handling) and light. Airis' "Angler" model is designed to be a more stable platform than their sport models, and might make a better choice if you can find one. Because it's not being manufactured any longer, their "Sport Tandem" would be an excellent choice as well. Any of these would be relatively easy to transfer to and from, and can be usually be configured as "single" or "tandem".

.Sevylor and some other companies also make SOTs that may work for you, but there is no "well" to sit in, and they may be a little too tippy to be able to transfer to and from without someone ending up in the water.

In the case of a person with limited abilities, quality is very important. We suggest that someone who has disabilities use the best possible kayak available to them.

A used kayak may be an excellent way to start while you develop your skill and determine what would be most useful for you. Be cautious and don't settle just for what's available. If it doesn't meet your needs, you'll be limited, frustrated, and worn out trying to adapt too much.

For the sake of clarity (and the photos we have) we'll discuss mainly the simplest and easiest to use type of kayak, the plastic paddle-propelled sit-on-top (when I wrote this, the kayaks I discussed previously were not available)

Stability

One of the most important aspects for the disabled is boat stability. There are two types of stability – primary and secondary. Primary has to do with "wobble" when the kayak is flat on still water that is corrected with shifts of balance. Secondary stability has to do with the amount of angle required to tip the boat over.

Each boat has unique characteristics. Your body type (length and size of your upper body, legs and arms) and function (how you maintain balance and what your abilities and limitations are) will determine how each boat works for you. Many paddlesport centers recognize the need to try out different models, and offer demos or rentals and expertise to help you choose what's best for you.

 Seating could be an important factor. Even for kayaks that have a regular seat or one molded in (on the hardshells) it might be a good idea to look at aftermarket seats that are available with extensive padding and adjustable lumbar and back support that can make a huge difference.

 Kayak weight could also be an important consideration. Out of the water any kayak can be heavy, clumsy, and difficult to carry. A mid-sized boat (9 – 13 ft., usually the best for a novice) may weigh 25 – 50 lbs (inflatables are generally lighter than hardshells). Only some have handles that actually help in carrying, and there has to be an appropriate way to get it to and from the water, and store it between uses.

 Color may be important if you think you'll be paddling in busy water. Yellow and orange are most highly visible, while blue and white (that may look like waves) are most difficult to see and may make you invisible to powered watercraft.

 Before you make a final decision on a kayak, look into what accessories and add-ons may be available. Manufacturers, outfitters, and even discount sites (i.e.eddyflower.com) have a huge variety of equipment for almost every need.

PFD

 A properly fitting Personal Flotation Device is essential for enjoying any time on the water. Choose the best you can afford, one that fits properly and will not interfere with your paddling effort. Make sure it says "Canoeing or Paddling" on the label. Then try it on, and see if the advertising is accurate.

Paddle

 There are all kinds of theories, equations, and opinions about what type of paddle is best for what kind of activity. They are generalities, and don't address any specific needs of someone who's disabled.

There are many factors to consider in choosing a paddle. How long are your arms and upper body? What kind of upper extremity strength and limitations do you have? How big is the kayak you'll be using, and under what conditions? What is your budget?

The basic rule is to use what fits and feels right for you.

Getting on the water

Know boat safety and local rules and regulations.

Become familiar with ways to reenter your kayak if you capsize; Mark Olson of Ocean Kayak (oceankayak.com) has an excellent maneuver he calls "BBF" – bellybutton, bottom, feet.

Make sure someone knows where you're going, and when you expect to be back

Be prepared!

Check on weather forecast and water conditions.

Have a waterproof bag with essentials in it:
> ID
>
> Cell phone or hand-held radio tuned to your local emergency frequency (if the radio is waterproof, attach it to your PFD.
>
> Camera (if wanted)
>
> Medications (if needed)
>
> Lip balm

Wear appropriate clothing. It can be cooler on the water than on land, so layer with polypropylene or fleece garments.

You need to carry a whistle (attached to your PFD).

Be sure you have a quality hat (preferably gore-tex), with plenty of coverage.

Flip flops are NOT appropriate kayaking apparel. Outdoor sandals or watershoes will provide quick-drying protection without retaining cold water.

Entering the kayak

Choose gradual sloping shore access. A beach is best. A

concrete boat ramp is often covered with algae - it can be steep, slick, and crowded with impatient boaters.

If you're using a walker, advance into the water until the kayak is just above knee level, and pivot into the cockpit. In one motion (if possible) sit in the seat as you swing your legs over the side into the cockpit.

If you're using a manual wheelchair roll the chair into the water until the seat is level with the kayak's gunwale. Position the wheelchair as you would for a chair-to-chair slide board transfer. Use a long slide board to stretch from the chair to the full width of the kayak to help prevent it from tipping.

Have assistants stabilize both the wheelchair and the kayak. If you only have one person with you, devise a way ahead of time to fasten your paddle across the kayak in an area that won't interfere with you entering or exiting. You can try slipping large foam blocks over the blades to act as outriggers to keep the kayak from tipping.

Transfer using the slide board as you normally would.

Notes:

Raise your feet into the kayak and position them in the foot wells. Secure your legs if necessary.

Settle to establish your balance with your assistant's help.

Before getting into deeper water paddle around in the shallows to become accustomed to the boat and movement.

Practice the reentry maneuver you explored beforehand.

Leaving the kayak
Position the wheelchair so that the seat is below the level of the kayak's gunwale.

Position the slide board for the transfer.

Reverse the entry process.

An alternative maneuver would be to move the kayak to deeper water. Exit the kayak by simply falling over the side to allow the PFD to support you in the water, and float to the chair. Note: Entering an inflatable is relatively easy, but transferring out can be difficult if the kayak isn't stiff enough to support the push-off. You can try deflating the air tube on the side you're transferring over, but that is rarely successful.

High-pressure inflatable kayak hulls (again, like the Airis "Angler") are rigid enough to a push-off, and the gunwale isn't so high as to be an insurmountable barrier.

Summary
Kayaking is not for everyone, but it can be enjoyable for a

lot more people than you might think. If you do try it, remember that the kayak you start out in may not be perfect for you, but it may give indications of what you need.

Kayak manufacturers like Airis, Ocean Kayak, Perception, Advanced Elements, Aire, and others can be valuable sources of information. Outfitters like NRS and discounters like Campmor have a wide range of accessories. Check locally to see if any of the nearby retailers or guides can help.

Excellent organizations like adaptive.org, Disabled Sports USA, and Live Strong can help with experience and direction to adapt to specific needs. There may also be local paddling clubs that can provide invaluable information, support, and paddling buddies.

Notes:

More Notes:

Kayak Fishing

Most of us started out fishing on the bank or dock and envying those guys out there in boats (we just *knew* they were catching so much more than we were).

You may not be willing or able to invest in a boat and motor, but an inflatable will get you out on the water with those guys and you can see if you've been missing anything.

One of the advantages of having a kayak is using it to get into places no one else can get to. You can be the guy they look at enviously as you slip into small coves or heavy brush.

But like everything else, safety should come first. There are certain things to always keep in mind when being in an inflatable while using very sharp objects. The less expensive and durable the kayak, the more careful you need to be to avoid a bad ending to a good day. Even a fish's fin may cause a puncture that sends you home or into the water.

Those tight coves or creek mouths you can sneak into may also have invisible submerged brush or branches that easily get you impaled – and stuck somewhere no one else can even see you, let alone get to you to help you get out. Whistle!

One drawback of using a kayak is that, while it may have plenty of storage, it may be difficult to get to what you need while out on the water. Everything you need should be within easy reach (without having to lean too far one way or another) so you need to carry minimal equipment. Think about where you might put that big tackle box that would be comfortable.

At kayakfishingtales.com (or all over YouTube) you can see video of how other fishermen have addressed different issues, and adapt their solutions to your own needs.

There are a growing number of specialized outfitters for kayak fishermen, like kayakfishing-gear.com and NRS.com.

It should go without saying that if you're going to be out on the water for any length of time you need to let someone know where you're going and when you plan to be back, and always go with a partner. You need a PFD, a hat with a broad brim, polarized sunglasses, sunscreen and protective clothing, and plenty of water.

If you don't have one, invest in a quality seat with plenty of back support. It will pay for itself many times over by saving you back pain and fatigue.

You can never have enough D-rings to attach gear and storage bags to for keeping everything secure. Elastic cord and aluminum clips (available from inflatableboats.com and other outfitters) can keep everything from going overboard. Remember – once it goes, it's gone. You can't very well go get it.

First, a "paddle keeper" (a nice glue-on one is available from Sea Eagle) will keep your paddle out of the way. It's very difficult to put a paddle anywhere else without risking it being in the way at the worst possible moment, or being knocked into the water, to float out of reach.

One manufacturer seems to have put this all together all in one package. Saturn makes a "Pro-Angler" model that can be a kayak or a canoe, has a *bunch* of D-rings, and all kinds of configurations to meet almost anyone's needs.

A vest with plenty of pockets would be very handy. A clipper on a lanyard would be much easier to use (and safer) than a knife on a belt sheath.

Canvas "boxes" like those used on personal pontoon boats can be velcroed to the top of a side air tube like they are with the pontoons to hold equipment.

Advanced Elements now has a kit for attaching a chrome rail in a kayak that can be used to mount a fish-finder, etc. and then be removed when it's not needed.

A longer rod (nine feet or longer) will help get fish around the bow of the boat while playing them, and help avoid getting open hooks too close to the boat. A cooler behind the seat with vertical plastic pipes attached to it can hold the rod when not in use (you can just reach back over your shoulder to grab it). One way to keep the rod from joining your paddle in the water is to attach it with an elastic cord to something. Two D-rings glued a foot or two apart to the lower part of the side tube (and out of your paddling zone) with an elastic cord stretched in between works well. Knot the elastic cord you've attached to your rod around the cord that's stretched between the D-rings so it can slip either way. You can also use a carabineer or some other clip to connect it.

Instead of a stringer, a mesh bag works well to keep your catch fresh and secure.

A net might be handy if you don't want your prize catch, slimy and cold as it is, flopping around between your legs.

Keep in mind as well that inflatables sit more on top of the water, and can be blown all over a lake by strong winds. A small anchor may be vital to keep you where you want to be.

If you want to be creative (and energetic), you can adapt

your kayak for trolling. There are some "glue-on" rod holders available, or you can find an inflatable raft designed for fishing that is no longer useful (trust me, they're not that hard to find). Make sure it has a rod holder used for trolling. Cut it out with a pair of fairly heavy scissors. Glue it just behind the seat of your kayak on top of the side tube so it's out of the way of your paddling effort, but easily reachable. You can use epoxy cement or, if you don't think you're going to encounter Moby Dick, a cheaper alternative would be to use DAP contact cement.

     Besides the rod holder, you can use the grommets and other pieces from the donor raft to make your kayak more user-friendly.

Notes:

Kayak Sailing

While at first it may not seem that "kayaking" and "sailing" would be associated, some of the most respected names in inflatable kayaking have made an excellent effort to make it possible.

The first big question is: "WHY?"

Kayaking is the ultimate non-intrusive sport. Using a sail would be even more zen-like than paddling.

Admit it: there's something very alluring about being able to lean back and allow the wind to propel you across the waves.

The downside is that you have to want to go the way the wind is blowing, and you usually have to paddle back.

Sea Eagle, Advanced Elements, and Windpaddle, among others, have developed small sails that mount on the bow of an inflatable kayak and are easily useable.

There are larger sails available, but in order to use them it's usually necessary to add pontoons or something similar to keep the kinetic energy generated by the sail from capsizing the kayak.

Hobie has also developed sails specifically for their inflatable kayaks, but their kayaks are generally much heavier than other inflatables for their length.

For $100 (Advanced Elements' RapidUp Sail Kit) or $160 (Sea Eagle's QuikSail) you can get a reasonably easy to set up and use sail that, while it won't set any speed records for you, will get you across the lake, or allow you to rest during a long paddle.

We haven't been able to personally evaluate any of these devices, but knowledgeable colleagues have used and liked them.

Each website has videos to demonstrate how to use them, and there are a growing number of videos on the Internet as well.

One caution: there are a greater number of sail kits available for hardshell kayaks. If you do decide to be adventurous, be sure the sail you choose is meant for an inflatable, and will mount on your kayak.

Kayak Pedaling

Hobie has managed to combine two athletic disciplines into one with their "Mirage Drive" apparatus – a pedal-driven form of propulsion.

The mechanism is actually inserted through the deck into the water. The pedals are above the deck and easily worked to provide the kinetic energy, and the blades are below the kayak to transfer the energy into forward momentum.

The blades come in several sizes for different demands. Because they extend below the kayak, working in shallow water can be tricky. The mechanism is easily pulled up and out of the way, but if you don't see a submerged rock or tree you could easily damage the blades.

Having said that, the people who use these kayaks tend to speak very highly of them.

They can fish while leaving their hands free, or just use the larger muscle groups in their legs for propulsion.

The kayaks themselves are stable (but rather heavy) and so can also be used for photography, birding, or any other activity that requires a stable platform.

Surf Kayaking

People have been using kayaks to play in the surf since someone tried sitting on a surfboard and paddling, and kept falling off. In the 70's someone tried solving the problem by adding the top of a conventional kayak to a surfboard. Kayaks specific to surf use have evolved since then to several very specific types.

As it becomes more popular, more manufacturers of inflatable kayaks have started making more specialized boats and changing marketing for the ones they've already made.

Depending on the surf conditions and the paddler's skill, many whitewater inflatable kayaks can be used in surf until the paddler can determine what most closely meets his/her needs.

If you're not interested in the more esoteric aspects of surf kayaking (like, describing sixteen different types of surf and the advantages of having a kayak ½ inches wider than another), then just take out what you've got and have at it. Enjoy yourself!

Surf kayaks tend to be shorter, similar to whitewater kayaks. Like whitewater kayaks, there also should be secure seating and ways to secure your lower body to the boat.

If your kayak has a closed cockpit, a spray skirt would be a great help to keep water out of your lap. If you have on open cockpit, a self-bailing boat would keep you from filling up with water and foundering.

Some of the same precautions need to be taken as you would in whitewater; others may not apply. You still need to be careful of sharp edges – not so much branches, but certainly glass and shells.

You should wear a well-fitting helmet and a high-quality PFD.

Shorter paddles tend to be more useful in surf. For the average paddler a 180 – 200 cm. length would probably be best.

There are more and more videos on youtube and other sites with information on surf kayaking. They're easily found, and can provide information that is impossible to do here.

Watch them, and be that much more prepared when you go

to the beach.

Notes:

Sea Kayaking

There are very few dedicated inflatable sea kayaks. Usually paddlers are asked to make due with something that can be adapted to somehow meet their needs.

Sea kayaks are longer and narrower than other kayaks to meet the specific demands of paddling in a very difficult environment over long distances. They're usually more than 13' to displace more water (to ride and float better) and narrower than the "normal" 33" – 36" of most inflatables. Tandems are common.

A closed cockpit is necessary to keep out the very cold water that is usual in big water, even in summer (the exception being the tropics).

A non-specific kayak can be used for short excursions in protected waters, but be very careful. Rogue waves, currents, and wind can be very problematic even when land is still in sight.

If you do decide to use a non- "sea kayak" you need to consider the environment. Large side tubes will help you bob over waves and keep out all but the worst of the waves. A good rocker (bow lift) will help you get over waves head-on.

Be sure you have something to remove any excess water from inside the kayak.

A self-bailing inflatable would not be a good choice. There may be a way to let excessive water out, but it also allows a constant level of sea water inside the kayak.

You *must* have adequate clothing to prevent hypothermia. Layers of clothing with polypropylene or fleece to wick away moisture would be best, with a waterproof outer layer (either specifically designed paddling clothing or a dry suit). Be sure to include gloves, booties, and a neoprene hood in case your hat isn't doing the job. A wide-brimmed Gore-tex hat works very well, or perhaps a sou'wester.

When you start planning your trip the first thing you should do is talk to the local authorities to get information on watercraft regulations, laws governing wildlife (i.e. here in Puget Sound there is very enthusiastic enforcement of laws regarding contact with orcas), and hazards and dangers you need to be aware of.

Selecting a kayak

You will need a deck that sheds water. If you can get the water to sluice off your kayak instead of collecting anywhere you will able to float, paddle, and change directions more easily.

Depending on your attitude towards kayaking, a bow that lifts over an oncoming wave (a pronounced rocker) rather than one that cuts through a wave (a knifing bow) will be less tiring.

A kayak with a pronounced rocker (lifting bow) will also help if you get caught between the curved back of one wave and curved front of another. If you have a kayak with very little rocker you may end up with the bow and stern buried in water while the center of the kayak is held above the water's surface.

Your kayak should be equipped with a high-visibility towline (preferably one that floats) in case you become exhausted or impaired.

Choosing a paddle

Paddling on large bodies of water usually entails many hours. A longer, narrower blade will not take as much effort to use for each stoke as a short, wide blade would. Your muscles would be more able to rest between efforts, so you would be able to paddle for long periods of time without becoming extremely fatigued.

Environmental Safety

Water and weather conditions can cause any number of serious, and sometimes life-threatening, problems.

Water temperature and tide conditions, impending inclement weather, and wind direction and speed all have to be checked before you venture out on big water.

Be conversant with nautical charts and carry the appropriate one with you.

Accessories

A compact bilge pump will help keep you from foundering by removing excess water from your kayak. A sea sock will help keep water from entering the kayak through the cockpit in heavy seas and will also help in case of a capsize.

A compass or a GPS will help keep you on track and determine where you are if need be.

Dry storage bags will keep essential equipment dry and safe. That equipment should include a first aid kit, a visual distress signal (flare gun), VHF hand-held radio, extra clothes, extra batteries, flashlight, medications, camera, and water.

An Emergency Position Indicating Radio Beacon (EPIRB) will transmit a beep continuously for up to 24 hours (as of this writing). It cannot receive or transmit voice, it can only indicate there is some kind of an emergent problem. They have become much more popular recently because of widely publicized incidents involving avalanche victims, and should be easier to find as they become used more.

A paddle leash will help keep your paddle with you, but you should also have a spare paddle of some kind tucked away just in case.

Kayaking over large bodies of water is a truly unique experience, but you have to be prepared to make sure your adventure is a memorable one for all the right reasons.
Notes:

More notes:

Cold Weather Kayaking

There's nothing like regaling your friends with lurid tales of your rugged adventures while kayaking in the dead of winter.

There's also nothing like freezing to death because you didn't prepare yourself properly for actually enjoy winter kayaking.

First, find someone who shares your proclivity for paddling in a truly hostile environment. *Never* kayak alone when the weather is cold or inclement.

Seriously evaluate the kayak you plan on using. The air bladders will help insulate you from the cold, but any contact with hard or jagged surfaces can cause serious damage to an otherwise durable PVC inflatable made brittle by the cold.

Paddle blades may also become brittle, and shatter if you have to use them to apply pressure during a push-off, causing you to overbalance and capsize.

Hypalon kayaks are less susceptible to being affected by the cold, but will be heavier and have different characteristics when cold from when they are warm.

Cold just by itself can be dangerous. Besides the well-known hazards of frostbite and loss of consciousness, dropping body temperature (hypothermia) can affect judgment, reflexes, and muscle function (that can then lead to frostbite, …….etc.).

Any immersion in freezing water will result in immediate hypothermia. Immersion causes a "gasp" reflex – if your face is underwater, you can suck freezing liquid straight into your lungs.

The first step in preparing for cold-weather paddling is getting as much information and training as possible. There are cold-weather classes in most colder areas, and on-line information is readily available.

Use the right equipment. Most inflatable kayaks have open cockpits. You need to use a kayak that has a cockpit that can be closed off with a spray skirt. There are several available – Sevylor's Pointer series, Advanced Elements has some excellent kayaks available. Aire, Tomcat, and others also make excellent kayaks that have closed cockpits.

Clothing needs to be layered, loose (so it doesn't impede any movement) and the outer layer needs to be waterproof (i.e. a quality drysuit). A wetsuit (even a cold-water suit) usually won't protect enough, and will compress any clothing underneath it, minimizing any insulating properties.

Neoprene gloves and boots will minimize any danger of frostbite, and, in the case of your hands, keep them gripping the paddle

A waterproof or water-shedding hood is also a necessity. An amazing amount of body heat can be lost through the top of your head (especially if you don't have as much hair as you used to).

Always carry extra clothing, chemical hand-warmers, and material to build a fire.

A marine radio will allow you to call for help.

Never go out on icy water without taking the classes and learning how to deal with things you might never think of as hazardous – like chunks of ice that may capsize you with just a nudge.

Other Inflatables

The basic principles I've discussed in the book apply to all inflatable watercraft.

The manufacturing processes, materials, and repair, transport, storage, and safety issues are all very similar.

Rafts

Just as with inflatable kayaks, there is a huge range of cost and durability when it comes to inflatable rafts, or boats. There is a much wider range of specialization for rafts. No matter what they are supposed to be designed for, or marketed as, some are good for paddling around close to shore on a calm lake, and some could

ride out a tsunami with aplomb.

It doesn't help that the number of occupants "certified" for some of these rafts would seem to be rather fantastical. You may be able to fit 4 adults in a 6 foot raft, but would you really want to? Or would you be able to do any kind of activity while all of you were crammed in there?

The smarter thing to do would be to find a raft large enough and durable enough to be appropriate and safe for what you want to use it for.

A sturdy raft (or even a flimsy one) may be safe enough for one adult who can swim and who will wear a quality PFD while using it on a calm lake. A $1000 raft made of hypalon or similar materials may be safe for one or a group of adults (again, wearing their PFD's at all times) rafting on a Class V river with an experienced guide.

Each situation is unique, and determines what safety rules (and common sense) must be followed for a safe day on the water.

Unfortunately, because they're much more widely available and involve more people, inflatable boats tend to be the subject of more news stories than any other watercraft.

People remember seeing large rafts blasting through huge rapids, the tourists conquering nature and grinning ear to ear. What they don't see is the guidance and protection by professionals and extremely durable raft material. They associate the indestructible raft they see on TV with the $80 boat they see in their grocery store.

Every year there are lurid stories in the headlines or on the 6 o'clock news about inflatables being involved in drownings. They may not present essential facts (what would be the fun in that?) like the 15 partygoers who happened to be in a 4 man inflatable they bought at the grocery store while they were buying beer. After lightening the load by several six-packs they floated off down the river (without life vests) until they brushed up against a submerged branch, tearing out the whole bottom of the boat and spilling the impaired crowd into ice-cold water.

It isn't always about alcohol, and not always about a river. It may be about any size boat over-crowded with kids at the lake for a picnic, close to shore so that no one thought that *life preservers* were necessary.

What seems to persist forever is that an inflatable was involved.

Personal Pontoon Boats

Personal pontoon boats are kind of a hybrid that has inflatable kayak-like air bladders to support a metal frame.

The composition and design of the frame becomes part of the durability equation. If the pontoons are made of very durable material and the frame is engineered to endure severe forces, the paddler can safely run Class V rapids if he or she has skill and experience. If the pontoons are made of material that does not resist punctures severe forces or the frame is flimsy, then the craft will not withstand the stresses of swift or rough river currents safely, and should be used in calm water only.

Float Tubes

The earliest versions were called "Belly Boats", so called because the earliest versions were constructed from truck tire inner tubes and you sunk down into them to your belly. Or your belly stopped you from going any further. Whichever.

The first one was probably conceived by someone overflowing with ingenuity (and probably beer). He must have thought it would be a great idea to tie a rope from one side of an inner tube to another to hold him up while he fished. It was simple, cheap, and he didn't have to share it with anybody and he didn't have to worry about falling out of the boat.

After about 10 minutes on the water he must have discovered that the idea of straddling that rope thing might have to be reconsidered. And he needed something to help move him through the water.

I'm sure his wife was happy to sew him a sling that worked so much better she was able to enjoy many days of peace and quiet.

Float tubes have evolved greatly since then. U-shaped air bladders are now encased in heavy-duty nylon, festooned with storage pockets, drink holders, cell phone holders and other amenities (and probably wi-fi someday soon). Some users have specially designed fins to help propel them around the water instead of the mundane swim fins you or I might use.

Fly fishermen are mainly responsibility for their development to today's excellent models. Most models cater to the specific needs of this group, with a stripping apron marked with a ruler to make sure they can measure their catch (and perhaps embellish the story later). They can also be found with holders for flies and lures.

Float tubes are small and light enough to carry to remote lakes and ponds for solitary fishing, photography, or birding and can be stored in a small duffel. They can be used on large lakes and deltas to get into areas others can't reach.

The one drawback is that you always have to remember that your lower half will be in the water all the time. Most fishermen use chest waders to maintain their comfort, while others might use the lower portion of a wet suit or a dry suit. Dress for cold conditions (at least from the waist down) and keep in mind the universal safety measures we've discussed in other parts of this book.

SUP's

Stand Up Paddleboards, or SUP's, have become increasingly popular.

They look kind of like an overly large surfboard, with a central surface for a person to stand on that allows the feet some traction. There's a single large paddle used to propel the user.

An inflatable paddleboard need to be rigid so it does not flex when the paddler stands on it. This is made possible with drop-stitch technology. It allows for high air pressure inside very tough materials, making the board extremely rigid.

With greater demand comes new technology, and in the future inflatable paddleboards (and other inflatables) will be lighter and more durable.

Notes:

Glossary

When folks start speaking "kayak" you'll want to know what the *hell* they're talking about.

Aft: Toward the back of the kayak.

Backpaddle: To paddle backwards, usually against a current.

Bailer: A scoop, cup, or hat used to remove water from a kayak. Or anyone who can be seen flinging water over the side as if their life depended on it. Great opportunity to offer to help. Or laugh, depending.

Beam: Widest part of the kayak. Or the paddler.

Bearing: The direction of an object or landmark.

Bilge: The transition area from the bottom to the side of a kayak or raft.

Blade: The flat part of the paddle.

Bow: The front end of the kayak.

Broach: Stuck against an obstacle by the force of the current.

Broadside: The position of the kayak perpendicular to the current, wind, or waves, presenting its broad side to natural forces.

Buoy: A floating device identifying a location, obstruction, hazard, or channel. Especially important if marking something like a 5mph. zone for power boats.

Capsize: Tip over.

Catch: The portion of the stroke where the blade enters the water.

Centerline: An imaginary line running the length of the kayak, dividing it into equal halves.

Clean: The portion of a river that is free of hazards and obstructions.

Coaming: The lip or edge that some inflatable kayaks have around the cockpit to hold a spray skirt.

Cockpit: The area where the paddler sits.

Course: The direction you want to go.

Cubic feet per second (CFS): A measurement of water flow. One CFS is how fast it takes 7.5 gallons of water to go past a given point in one second.

Current: Moving water.

Deck: The top half of the kayak. Or the bottom half if you happen to be upside down.

Depth: The distance between the gunwale or deck and the bottom of the kayak at a specified point.

Draft: The vertical distance between the waterline and the deepest part of the kayak.

Dry suit: Waterproof outermost layer of clothing with watertight seals at the neck, wrist, and ankle. Expensive, but absolutely necessary if you're going to be out in cold weather or water.

Ebb: A receding tide. Opposite of flood tide.

Eskimo roll: Maneuver using body movement and paddle stroke to turn a capsized kayak upright. Most effective with closed cockpit kayaks.

Estuary: The area along a coastline where freshwater meets saltwater.

Face: Area of the paddle blade that pushes against the water. Usually has manufacturer's name on it so you can tell the difference and don't look stupid using it the wrong way.

Fathom: Six feet.

Feathered: Paddle blades set at an angle to each other to aid paddling, cut down wind resistance. If you can paddle so fast you have to worry about wind resistance, you don't need to be reading this.

Flatwater: Water without rapids, such as a lake, sheltered bay, or slow-moving river.

Flood tide: Incoming tide. Opposite of ebb tide.

Footbrace: A support for a paddler's feet to brace against, to increase the effectiveness of a paddler's effort and/or help secure him/her in the kayak.

Forward: Toward the bow from the cockpit.

Freeboard: The distance from the waterline to the lowest part of the side tube, usually dependant on the paddler's weight and gear. Too large a paddler for the kayak, and/or too much gear, see "swamp".

Gradient: Measures the rate of a river's drop by the number of feet it descends in one mile. Very important in determining the speed of the current you might expect.

Grip: The area where a paddler holds the paddle. Or where your terrified passenger is holding on for dear life ("No really, you'll *love* it once you get out there!")

Gunwale: The top edge of the side tube of an inflatable.

Hardshell: Kayak with hull made of thermoplastic/PVC (inexpensive, easy to shape into almost anything), fiberglass, or carbon fiber (expensive, very light and rugged).

Heading: The direction you're going, as you're opposed to the direction you're supposed to be going.

Hip Snap: A maneuver using a sudden jerk of torso and knee to change the angle of a kayak.

Huli: Hawaiian for capsizing. Not to be confused with "hula", which also occurs if you've been celebrating too much.

Hull: The bottom half of the kayak. (see "deck"). The part of an inflatable kayak most often impaled on submerged branches that you thought couldn't *possibly* be there.

Hypothermia: Potentially lethal lowering of core body temperature.

Keel: A strip that runs down the center of the hull from bow to stern.

Lee: The side away from the direction the wind is blowing.

Life vest: Also know as PFD, or pain in the butt when she makes you wear it. Too bad. Wear it and set a good example.

Numbass: What happens on a long trip when your custom seat comes between you and that soft inflatable floor you were anticipating. Think ahead!

Painters: Lines at the bow and stern that can be used to tow or be towed to shore. Or hopefully catch your kayak as it slides out into the river.

PFD: See "life vest", and read the whole chapter.

Port: The left side of a kayak or boat, facing forward.

Primary stability: how resistant a kayak is to tipping when it's flat on still water. Inflatables inherently have more primary stability than hardshells because of their structure (side tubes).

Put-in: The point from which you launch.

PVC: Short for polyvinyl chloride, a type of plastic that most inexpensive kayaks are made of. May be sandwiched with polyester or nylon to make a much more durable material.

Riffles: light, shallow rapids in Class I rivers.

Rocker: The profile of a keel from bow to stern. The greater the curve, the better turning ability. The flatter the profile, the better tracking. A banana would turn quickly, wouldn't paddle in a straight line for nothin'.

Rudder: Moveable blade-like structure (similar to skeg) that helps maintain directional stability and change direction.

Usually moved by foot pedals.

Secondary stability: How much resistance there is to tipping the kayak from side to side.

Shaft: The long tube connecting the blades of the paddle that you hold as you paddle. Can be plastic (cheap), aluminum (sometimes easily bent), fiberglass (durable), or carbon-fiber (light, expensive, upper crust/ something to casually brag about).

Skeg: Blade-like apparatus that aids directional stability.

Sleigh ride: what happens when a fisherman hooks a *big* fish (or passing ferry, powerboat, etc.)

Splash cover: A fabric cover over the open parts of an open cockpit to keep water out. Similar to a spray skirt.

Spoon: The amount of curvature or "scoop" in the face of the paddle's blade.

Starboard: The right side of a kayak or raft, facing forward.

Stern: The back end of the kayak. The last part you're going to see if you don't get the painter in time.

Strake: Short, long structure on bottom of kayak to aid in directional stability and durability (can help protect hull when contacting objects or ground)

Swamp: To fill a kayak or raft with water.

Sweep stroke: Used to turn your kayak by reaching ahead and out, then "sweeping" in a wide arc.

Swim beer: What a rescued swimmer usually buys for his/her rescuer as thanks (and to ensure future rescues).

Taco: What your kayak does if it's not inflated enough or you're too big for it. Much to the amusement of those around you, as it sinks under you the ends come up and meet above your head, perhaps with only an arm or leg sticking out.

Take-out: The end point of a trip, where you take your kayak out of the water.

Tandem: A kayak designed for two people.

Track: To go in a straight line.

Trim: The bow-to-stern balance of the kayak. Adjusted for optimal paddling.

Tupperware: plastic/PVC kayak, canoe, other watercraft.

Waterline: The level that the water reaches on a kayak or raft hull when it is in the water. A heavily loaded watercraft will ride lower in the water and be more susceptible to water coming over the gunwale.

Weather cocking: the phenomenon that causes the stern to swing around to one side or another when you stop paddling. The bow has water pressure to press on the tip and on either side to hold it on a straight course, the stern will swing to overcome resistance.

Wetsuit: Very tight neoprene suit that traps water next to the skin, providing insulation. Wetsuits come in several thicknesses, so be careful you don't get one meant for arctic conditions.

Wigwag: What your bow does if you paddle too hard or don't have any skegs or strakes to help you track correctly.

Printed in Great Britain
by Amazon.co.uk, Ltd.,
Marston Gate.

Kayaking is not some mystical skill, or limited to those gifted few. Any of us who are "athletically challenged" can enjoy a day or a week on the water alone or with our families and friends without being an expert or spending a fortune.

To do that, you have to be prepared with the right knowledge and equipment.

This book is a comprehensive, non-technical guide to choosing an inflatable kayak, using it safely, and taking care of it so it will last you for years to come.

Barb Roth is a native of western Washington, where kayaking is something of a religion. She always wanted to kayak, but her class with a hardshell was "disappointing" and she gave up her dream. Then she was introduced to inflatables, and has be an avid kayaker ever since.

Kevin Perry has been her partner for 8 years, and introduced her to inflatables. He's been using inflatable kayaks for river rescue and recreation since 1979.

ISBN 9781496195043

9 781496 195043

90000